# THE HIGHER LEARNING
# IN AMERICA

The Storrs Lectures
delivered at Yale University

# The
# Higher Learning
# in America

BY

ROBERT MAYNARD HUTCHINS

NEW HAVEN AND LONDON
YALE UNIVERSITY PRESS

Copyright 1936 by Yale University Press
Thirteenth printing, September 1967
Printed in the United States of America by the
Carl Purington Rollins Printing-Office of the
Yale University Press, New Haven, Connecticut.

TO
CHARLES E. CLARK

# CONTENTS

# CONTENTS

# Preface to the Paperbound Edition

THIS BOOK was written twenty-five years ago, during the Great Depression, when Russia was a backward nation, when colonialism was in flower, and when people in the advanced industrial countries still believed that technology could menace neither their livelihood nor their lives.

This was before television, before World War II, before the United Nations, before the Cold War, before the Affluent Society, before the Hydrogen Bomb, before the forty-hour week, and before the rise and fall of the labor unions. It was before oligopolistic arrangements among giant corporations superseded competition as the distinguishing characteristic of our economic system, and before American culture became bureaucratic. It was another world.

In that world, education did not enjoy the standing or command the interest that it does today. The Horatio Algers of the nineteenth century used to boast that they had carved out their careers without

benefit of book learning. An early article by Walter
Gifford, then a vice-president of A. T. and T., sought
to show that the more education you have, the more
money you make, and created a sensation. It may
have started the turning of the tide. By 1936 the tide
was running fast, but it had not yet overwhelmed
the higher learning. All that it had done was to create
strain, stress, and confusion.

In 1936 research was having a hard time in the
American university. People could understand the
idea of teaching; they understood at least that young
people had to be prepared to make a living. But the
mystique of science had not yet covered the earth.
That had to await the demonstration of the ability
of scientists to blow up the world. Government and
business were largely indifferent to education. They
did not finance it, because they saw no reason why
they should. Their only interest, expressed through
the hit-and-run activities of minor demagogues on
the fringes, was in keeping teachers from arousing
the students to any desire for social change. Senator
Joseph McCarthy and the rash of loyalty oaths and
investigations were yet to come.

Now, things are changed. Everybody wants an education, or at least a degree. The time will arrive

shortly when no positions above manual labor will be open to those who are without the magic parchment. Vast sums, unheard of in my day, are sought and obtained in the name of education. An increasing fraction of this money comes from government and business. And most of it, of course, goes for what is called research. Today whatever is done in a university that cannot be called teaching is called research.

The universities in fact are now engaged in three activities that are not very closely related to one another: research, vocational certification, and social accommodation. Research requires no further explanation, although it should be said that one who wants the universities to be centers of independent thought may well be alarmed at the conscious or unconscious lapses from independence that large-scale support from government and business may induce. The universities have demonstrated their willingness to do almost anything for money. Government and business are not wholly disinterested in their approaches to the universities: they are not seeking the truth, but are hiring universities to promote the ends they have in view. If the truth serves these ends, it is merely a coincidence. As every university president knows, the receipt of any money, even a tuition fee, creates or is assumed to create an obligation—the larger the sum, the greater the obligation.

All occupations want to raise their social standing and limit competition. An easy way to do this is to get a law passed providing that no one may enter the occupation unless he has a degree from a school that purports to train neophytes for the occupation. Many so-called professional programs exist in order to provide the certification that these laws require. The content is not important; the point is that the student must serve his time. Schools of education, which have developed no content but which are the indispensable avenues to teaching positions in the elementary and secondary schools, offer an obvious and notorious example.

The young have to be accommodated until we are ready to have them go to work. That stage is being postponed to a later and later age, partly because we think they will be more successful as they have more education, partly because there are real pressures to keep people off the labor market by allowing them a shorter working life, and partly because it is now the fashion to go to college. If a young person goes to college because it is the thing to do or because there is nowhere else for him to go, the chances are not good that he will have any purpose in going there that is compatible with the purpose that a college ought to have. Nor, in the present state of curricula, is it at all likely that he will discover one in the course of his studies.

One of the easiest things in the world is to assemble a list of hilarious courses offered in the colleges and universities of the United States. Such courses reflect the total lack of coherent, rational purpose in these institutions. If the colleges and universities ever gave intellectual leadership to the United States, or if they ever trained their students to give such leadership to their fellow citizens, all serious claims to either have now been abandoned. Higher learning has disintegrated because American educational standards have collapsed—70 per cent of the colleges in the country offer "Remedial English"—and because specialism, vocationalism, and triviality have taken over. The question may now be solemnly asked whether, since these tendencies seem irreversible, it would not be better to forget about most of our existing colleges and universities and plan new institutions that would undertake the overwhelmingly important task that the colleges and universities have given up.

About the only statement of the purpose of education on which our people seem to agree is that it must help us to "keep ahead of Russia." Since the strength of Russia appears to lie in science and technology, the thing to do is to build up these aspects of higher learning. We also hear occasionally that since the Russians are seducing foreigners, we should teach Americans other languages so that we can be as successful with foreigners as the Russians.

But the object of the American educational system should be to help the American people become as intelligent as they can. Science should be a part of the education of every American, not because we can't otherwise compete with Russia but because we can't otherwise educate an intelligent man. And on one point the young author of this book was certainly wrong: he had a wholly inadequate view of the purpose of instruction in foreign languages. Every American should receive such instruction because without it he cannot understand what a language is. If he can never get outside his mother tongue, which he has unconsciously absorbed, he cannot grasp the structure of any language, including his own.

It is altogether likely that if the American people are as intelligent as they can be, they will be ahead of Russia. But if they base their educational program on the desire to stay or get ahead of Russia, they are surrendering their educational destiny to Russia and putting in her hands the determination of the kind of people Americans are to be.

Lest these animadversions on the loss of leadership and purpose seem the embittered reflections of a battle-scarred veteran of the academic wars, I quote from the current issue (summer 1961) of *New University Thought*. First, from an article by Gabriel Breton, Assistant Professor at Monteith College:

> We have . . . witnessed the disappearance of the university as the locus of thought and universalism and its replacement by the fragmented academic underworld and the birth of a new class, the academic menials, which is on the way to becoming the most conservative force in the society . . . Devotion to technique and technology *per se* has become, for many academicians, a form of commitment in itself. Technique, in

the academic sub-universe, is a ritual. I believe that the reason for this state of affairs lies at the heart of the present madness and apathy. It is the all-consuming fear of the intellectuals to define ends and goals . . . The furor for impartiality and objectivity—or that sort of conservatism of the liberals—is also nothing other than the refusal to formulate precise ends, because the consequences will be . . . a confrontation with the necessity of a total conversion of our cultural mystique. This implies, first of all, the acceptance in principle of the necessity for the transcultural morality. It also implies that academic mores be placed under scrutiny. We would thus see that the academic world is incapable of working in the direction of a total conversion of the cultural mystique, since this institution is intimately involved in the basic structure of the culture.

Or listen to Ralph Nicholas, a graduate student in anthropology, writing in the same issue of the same publication:

To refer to these students who have come to college merely because they can afford it as "time-wasters" is not totally accurate. They have come in order to acquire certain skills which they will find essential in later life. Some of these skills are acquired in "academic" classes. Technical abilities are frankly secondary, however, to those acquired in the fraternity house, formal balls, stags, and other social occasions in which the "student" learns how to talk business with those who have undergone a similar "education." It is not facetious to say that more than 50 per cent of what such "students" need to learn could as well be taught by a few months in a good country club. The rest is admittedly appropriate to classroom teaching, but it is not fit fare for a university.

Mr. Nicholas goes on:

The business community is the major beneficiary of the education of the middle- and upper-class students. The liberal arts and business administration graduates staff its offices and sales forces; the science graduates run its laboratories. Of the four principal varieties of professional schools—business, law, education, and medicine —two, law and business, are feeding personnel at a growing rate into "middle management" and junior chambers of commerce . . . The business community is prepared to pay for the kind of training it needs with substantial endowments and subsidies for special programs . . . Like the community of rich students, the business community is able to get what it wants from American colleges and universities because it can pay for it . . . "The needs of the community," as seen by university public relations men, include the needs of just about every community except the one which, presumably, cares most about education—the academic community. Through sheer demoralization, this community has lost one of its essential characteristics, its sense of unity. . . . The institutions of higher education in the United States ought to represent one aspect of an integrated community. A community of teachers, researchers, students, and others whose work involves the proposition that knowledge is a value, is socially useful and, in order to flourish, must have an independent social basis.

What of the future? In a country from which the advance of technology is slowly driving work as we

have understood it, in a world in which we may find
—if we survive—that we do not know what to do with
our goods or with ourselves, in an age in which only
intelligence and character of an unusual sort can prevent the final catastrophe, "we must as a people,"
says J. D. Williams, the mathematician of the RAND
Corporation, "achieve a new level of intellectual competence." Yet, he continues, "we have recently placed
most of our school systems in the hands of people
preoccupied with physical culture, togetherness, and
intellectually trivial curricula."

The old writer of this new preface agrees with
the young author of this book, when he says in his
last sentence, "Upon education our country must pin
its hopes of true progress, which involves scientific
and technological advance, but under the direction
of reason; of true prosperity, which includes external
goods but does not overlook those of the soul; and
of true liberty, which can exist only in society, and
in a society rationally ordered." Let us hope that we
can muster the imagination and courage to get education for our country before it is too late.

R. M. H.

*August 1961*

# THE HIGHER LEARNING IN AMERICA

## I. EXTERNAL CONDITIONS

IN the first of these chapters I propose to consider the external conditions under which American education operates. In the second I shall discuss the peculiar difficulties of universities, and especially of professional schools. In the third I shall suggest what a general education is, and in the fourth what a university might be.

The most striking fact about the higher learning in America is the confusion that besets it. This confusion begins in the high school and continues to the loftiest levels of the university. The high school cannot make up its mind whether it is preparing students for life or for college. Its student population is miscellaneous and variegated. The course of study is substantially uniform for all groups, whether they are prospective scientists, lawyers, clerks, or laboring men, and is apparently adjusted to the needs of only the smallest of these groups, that destined for the higher learning.

The junior college is in most places an extension of the high-school curriculum, which is there applied to an essentially similar though somewhat smaller student body. Here also the question whether the students are completing their education or are preparing to go on to the university has not been settled, and the aims of the institution are not clear.

The college of liberal arts is partly high school, partly university, partly general, partly special. Frequently it looks like a teacher-training institution. Frequently it looks like nothing at all. The degree it offers seems to certify that the student has passed an uneventful period without violating any local, state, or federal law, and that he has a fair, if temporary, recollection of what his teachers have said to him. As I shall show later, little pretense is made that many of the things said to him are of much importance.

The university is distinguished from the college by two things: professional schools and the Ph.D. degree. At present we do not know why the university should have professional schools or what they should be like. We do not even know what the professions are. Professional education consists either of going through motions that we have inherited or of making gestures of varying degrees of wildness that we hope may be more effectual. The Ph.D. degree, because it has become a necessary part of the insignia

of the college or university teacher, has lost any
other meaning. But universities also do research and
hope to train research men. The same degree is
awarded in recognition of research. The students
who are going to be teachers are put through a pro-
cedure which was designed to produce investigators.
The classes, the courses, the content, and the aims of
graduate work are as confused as those of the high
school.

For the sake of abbreviation I have of course ex-
aggerated the plight of the higher learning. It has,
in fact, many admirable qualities, not the least of
which is its friendly reception of anybody who
would like to avail himself of it. But we who are devoting our lives to it should learn something from
the experience of recent years. Up to the onset of the
present depression it was fashionable to call for more
and more education. Anything that went by the
name of education was a good thing just because it
went by that name. I believe that the magic of the
name is gone and that we must now present a defensible program if we wish to preserve whatever we
have that is of value. Our people, as the last few
years have shown, will strike out blindly under economic pressure; they will destroy the best and pre-

serve the worst unless we make the distinction between the two somewhat clearer to them.

If then the problem is to clarify the higher learning, let us examine the causes of its confusion. The first of them is very vulgar; it is the love of money. It is sad but true that when an institution determines to do something in order to get money it must lose its soul, and frequently does not get the money. Money comes to education in three ways—from students, from donors, and from legislatures. To frame a policy in order to appeal to any one of the three is fatal, and, as I have suggested, often futile as well. How much of the current confusion in universities would have been eliminated if boards of trustees had declined gifts which merely reflected the passing whims of wealthy men? Few restricted gifts have ever been made to a university that paid the expense of receiving them. If men are supported, they are not housed or given the books and equipment they need. If buildings are given, they are not maintained. If they are maintained, they are not manned. From the financial standpoint alone the university may be worse off after the gift than it was before. And from the educational or scientific standpoint it is likely to be unbalanced and confused. Dependence on the casual interests of donors means that nobody can tell from one year to another what a university's policy is. It will become next year whatever somebody is willing to pay to make it. I do not mean, of course, that universities do not need money and that they should not try to get it. I mean only that they should have an educational policy and then try to finance it, instead of letting financial accidents determine their educational policy.

Even more important is the influence on educational policy of student fees. It is probably fair to say that American universities above the junior year ought to do anything and everything that would reduce their income from students. This is true because most of the things that degrade them are done to maintain or increase this income. To maintain or increase it the passing whims of the public receive the same attention as those of millionaires. If the public becomes interested in the metropolitan newspaper, schools of journalism instantly arise. If it is awed by the development of big business, business schools full of the same reverence appear. If an administration enlarges the activities of the federal government and hence the staff thereof, training for the public service becomes the first duty of the universities. Today public administration, housing, forestry, and aëronautics are the absorbing subjects of university interest, just as international relations after the war was the topic to which we were to devote ourselves. At any moment crime, divorce, child labor, socialized medicine, or the corruption of lawyers may through some sensational incident become the most pressing problem of the higher learning. During the synthetic excitement of last year about communism, socialism, and other forms of redness, it suddenly became the duty of the colleges and universities to give courses in the eradication of these great evils and in the substitution for them of something called Americanism.

Undoubtedly the love of money and that sensitivity to public demands that it creates has a good deal to do with the service-station conception of a university. According to this conception a university must make itself felt in the community; it must be constantly, currently felt. A state university must help the farmers look after their cows. An endowed university must help adults get better jobs by giving them courses in the afternoon and evening. Yet it is apparent that the kind of professors that are interested in these objects may not be the kind that are interested either in developing education or in advancing knowledge. Since a university will not be able to have two kinds of professors and at the same time remain clear as to what it is about, it must follow that extension work can only confuse the institution.

Little more can be said in justification of the attempt to teach freshmen and sophomores under the same roof and with substantially the same staff as are employed for research and graduate and professional study. Unless we exclude from the first two years all students who are not likely to be scholars and professional men or who deserve unusual opportunities for the cultivation of the mind, we must confuse an institution which should be primarily devoted to scholarship, professional education, and the training of the mind. In most state universities, at least, no pretense is made that freshmen and sophomores are material for the kind of intellectual work that a university should sponsor. Here their presence is accounted for by a notion of democracy that I shall refer to later. In endowed institutions, however it may be rationalized, their presence is accounted for by the love of money. The university would lose income if it lost them. And since they are much less expensive than their elders and pay the same or higher fees, the loss of net income would be out of proportion to their number or the total fees they pay. Without these students, too, the whole apparatus of athletics, fraternities, and social life would have to be radically revised, and the voices of alumni would be raised in howls of anguished grief.

The presence of freshmen and sophomores leads to one of two results, both of them bad. On the one hand, the university may become an overgrown college where the success of a professor is determined by his ability to keep students awake and his extra-curriculum influence on their morals and manners. In such an institution the guiding star of educational policy is what the students say or even what the student paper says. On the other hand, the university may exploit the freshmen and sophomores, placing them in the hands of graduate students, who are given teaching posts instead of fellowships. In these circumstances promotion depends upon research; an interest in the problem of teaching undergraduates may be a definite liability. A university that attempts to do freshman and sophomore work therefore ends up doing either a poor university job or a poor col-

lege job. And one or the other of these situations ob-
tains at almost every American university today.

There is only one way that I have been able to
think of in which a university can entertain freshmen and sophomores and do well by them and by its
university obligations at the same time. That is to
take the view that the university may well try to
help the system of public education by working out
for it what a general education ought to be. A general education, I believe, should be given between
the junior year in high school and the end of the
sophomore year in college. I do not see how the public schools are ever going to command the time and
intelligence to develop the organization and content
appropriate to general education. I can see how a
university faculty might interest itself in the problem and accelerate a solution of it.

But even with such a hope and such an attitude
the complexities of operating the first two years in a
university are very serious. In the first place, few universities are so situated as to be interested or influ-
ential in the problems of public education. For those
who are not so situated the only answer is the abolition of the freshman and sophomore years. In the

second place, even if a university is so situated as to develop a scheme for public education, it is doubtful whether it should do so. A university has enough trouble with the problems of the higher learning. Taking on the burden of philanthropic work, no matter how valuable, can only diminish its effectiveness in its proper field.

By one method such philanthropy can perhaps be conducted without this sad result: the faculty dealing with general education must be independent of and even isolated from the university, close enough to it to get the advantages of its facilities and a few of its men; remote enough from it to be able to work on its problems without the interference or control of the university faculty and without interfering with or controlling that faculty. It remains to be seen whether any such organization can ever be effected and if so whether it can succeed. Nothing short of it can bring order out of the confusion produced by the conflicting aims of collegiate and university work.

The love of money means that a university must attract students. To do this it must be attractive. This is interpreted to mean that it must go to unusual lengths to house, feed, and amuse the young. Nobody knows what these things have to do with the higher learning. Everybody supposes that students think they are important. The emphasis on athletics and social life that infects all colleges and universities has done more than most things to confuse these institutions and to debase the higher learning in America.

It is supposed that students want education to be amusing; it is supposed that parents want it to be safe. Hence the vast attention given by universities at enormous expense to protect the physical and moral welfare of their charges. Parents must feel that their children are in good hands. It makes no difference whether those hands are already full. The faculty must be diverted from its proper tasks to perform the uncongenial job of improving the conduct and the health of those entrusted to it.

The love of money leads to large numbers, and large numbers have produced the American system of educational measurement. Under this system the intellectual progress of the young is determined by the time they have been in attendance, the number of hours they have sat in classes, and the proportion of what they have been told that they can repeat on examinations given by the teachers who told it to them. Such criteria as these determine progress from one educational unit to another, and are the basis for entrance to and graduation from professional schools. Since it is clear that these criteria are really measures of faithfulness, docility, and memory, we cannot suppose that they are regarded as true indications of intellectual power. They are adopted because some arbitrary automatic methods are required to permit dealing with large masses of students, and these methods are the easiest. Any others would compel us to think about our course of study and to work out ways of testing achievement in it. But large numbers leave us no time to think.

The love of money makes its appearance in universities in the most unexpected places. One would look for it in presidents and trustees. One would think that the last place one could hear it mentioned would be in faculty meeting. On the contrary, a good many professors instantly react to any proposal for the improvement of education by displaying a concern for the university's income that is notably absent when they are pressing for increases in their own research budgets. Two answers are usually made when any such suggestion is advanced: it is said that the students cannot do the work and that the university by frightening away students will reduce its income. What these answers usually mean is that the professors who make them do not want to change the habits of their lives. Since this cannot be made a matter of public knowledge, some philanthropic reason must be put forward instead.

Actually students will respond to a program designed to give them a better education. It usually happens that after the horrid predictions of professors in these cases more and better students desire to enroll, and specifically because of the innovation that was expected to scare them off. This has happened in my own experience with honors courses, general courses, general examinations, and the abolition of course credits and of the requirement of attendance at classes.

Even more important than the love of money as a cause of our confusion is our confused notion of democracy. This affects the length, the content, and the control of education. According to this notion a student may stay in public education as long as he likes, may study what he likes, and may claim any degree whose alphabetical arrangement appeals to him. According to this notion education should be immediately responsive to public opinion; its subject matter and methods may be regulated in great detail by the community, by its representatives, or even by its more irresponsible members.

What determines the length of free education for all? The answer is economic conditions. When there was a scarcity of men and a multiplicity of jobs it was limited to a very short time. Even Thomas Jefferson proposed that it should be confined to three years in the grades. Adam Smith reminds us that in the American colonies a widow with four children was a brilliant match because her offspring would begin so early to make their contribution to the family treasury. Those happy days are gone forever. Now we can hope to solve the problem of the unemployed adult only by removing the adolescent and the superannuated from the labor market. The superannuated may perhaps devote themselves to reflection and advice. The adolescent cannot. Some kind of activity will have to be found for them.

Up to date we have found only education and the Civilian Conservation Corps. The Civilian Conservation Corps I regard as a somewhat confused extension of the educational system. It is an attempt to meet the defects of that system. The principal defect of that system is that it makes almost no provision for pupils who cannot or will not learn from books. The Civilian Conservation Corps does, as to one sex at least, do something to meet this need. Sometime it may learn to do it better. The chief weakness of the Corps as an adjunct of the educational system is the absence of any intelligible basis for the selection of its members. If at present schools are for those who can learn by traditional methods and the CCC is for those who cannot, it should follow that the CCC should release to the schools those who can learn by traditional methods and the schools should release to the CCC those who cannot.

I hope, of course, that the methods of the schools may improve and that they will discover how to communicate an education to those who cannot read. As they make this discovery the numbers in the CCC may diminish. But I am clear that under present economic conditions some kind of educational or semieducational activity must be provided for the young up to approximately their twentieth year. If the depression lifts, we shall be in the same position; for the technological advances of recent years suggest that industry will require in the future proportionately fewer workers than ever before.

Economic conditions, then, determine the length

of free education for all; and present and prospective economic conditions are such that the terminus of the public education which the ordinary youth is expected to enjoy will be set at about the end of the sophomore year in college. This means that the public junior college will become the characteristic educational institution of the United States, just as the public high school has been up to now.

I may digress at this point to say that when the junior college has become the characteristic educational institution of the United States, universities and colleges which have insisted on maintaining a four-year course beginning with the freshman year and leading to the Bachelor's degree will find themselves somewhat embarrassed. We may expect to see a junior college wherever there is a high school today. There are already 450 of them, public and private, in this country. Eighty-five per cent of the public ones are in high-school buildings. They will therefore find it easy to take over the last two years of high school and develop a four-year unit devoted to general education. Under these circumstances we may expect the ordinary youth to stay at home and complete the work of the sophomore year in college. He will not go away to the university, if he goes at

all, until the junior year. Universities and colleges
which begin their work with the freshman year will
find their freshmen and sophomores limited to local
students and those who are rich enough to leave
home at a tenderer age than usual.

Already this process has gone very far. Analysis of
the domiciles of the freshmen at almost any American college or university will show that at least 75
per cent of them come from an area within 100 miles
of the institution. The proposed prize awards of the
University of Rochester and the national scholar-
ships at Harvard are attempts to minimize this situation. They will be unsuccessful; for they are against
the inevitable and the desirable trend of American
education. Universities may expect to have an over-
whelming proportion of local students in their freshman and sophomore years; and they may expect the
number of freshmen and sophomores to decline in
relation to the total enrollment. Of the students who
received the Bachelor's degree at the University of
Chicago last year 64.3 per cent, or almost two-thirds,
had attended one or more other institutions. Hence
it is folly for us to talk about the freshman and
sophomore years as preparation for later work; it is
folly to discuss a four-year program of education be-

ginning with the freshman year; and it is highly important that we should develop ourselves and encourage the junior colleges to develop an intelligible scheme of general education under which the student may either terminate his formal education at the end of the sophomore year or go on to university work.

But to return to democracy in education, you will observe that neither economic conditions nor anything else compels us to lengthen the span of public education for all beyond the end of the sophomore year in college. Free education should exist beyond this level, and exist in a fuller, richer form. But it should be open only to those who have demonstrated their ability to profit by it. It is perhaps the highest function of the state to provide opportunities for the development of scholarship, the improvement of the professions, and the cultivation of the mind. It can only debase these objects and prevent their attainment if it permits the children of taxpayers to wander at will through the higher learning. Under these circumstances university degrees cease to have any meaning and universities, indeed, cease to exist.

Our notion of democracy leads us to the view that

everybody is entitled to the same amount and to the same kind of education. This is reflected in our national passion for degrees, a passion which the late Barrett Wendell hoped to assuage by conferring the Bachelor's degree on every American citizen at birth. My judgment is that we cannot expect students who should leave at the end of the sophomore year to depart in peace unless that degree is conferred upon them at that time.

If we confer it at that time, what shall it represent? It should represent a good general education. We do not know what a good general education is. We do not know how to communicate it to those who cannot read. We must find out the answers to both these questions. It is possible that if we can discover what a general education is the problem of communication may partially solve itself; for it might be that the first fruits of an intelligible curriculum would be an interest in understanding it, even on pain of doing so through books. Democracy should mean that this curriculum from beginning to end is open to everybody. Adjustments to individual capacities should be made by permitting the student to proceed at his own pace, taking the examinations whenever in his opinion he is ready to take them.

Democracy does not require, however, that the higher learning should be open to anybody except those who have the interest and ability that independent intellectual work demands. The only hope of securing a university in this country is to see to it that it becomes the home of independent intellectual work. The university cannot make its contribution to democracy on any other terms.

The independent intellectual activity of universities is threatened by another consequence of our confusion about democracy, that which results from our confusion about democratic control. I will admit that the aims, methods, and subject matter of American education are so ill-defined that anybody might think that he could do better with it. Still one shudders to note that every citizen entertains the conviction that he is an educational expert of the most significant variety. In public institutions the financial control of the community is undoubted. But it is one thing to say how much money the community can spend on education and quite another to say how it shall be spent. The duly constituted representatives of the public may properly decide that the total expense of a state university must be cut. The decision as to which items should be reduced must rest with educators. In endowed institutions the interest of the community is in seeing to it that the corporation obeys the law. If the community doesn't like the conduct of the corporation, it may adopt legislation requiring changes in it. But an endowed university cannot modify its educational policies because newspaper editors are trying to increase their circulation or politicians their influence at its expense.

Academic freedom is simply a way of saying that we get the best results in education and research if we leave their management to people who know something about them. Attempts on the part of the public to regulate the methods and content of education and to determine the objects of research are encroachments on academic freedom. Attempts to control the private lives and public expressions of professors are of another order. They are attempts to interfere with the liberty of the citizen. The democratic view that the state may determine the amount of money to be spent on education and may regulate education and educators by law has nothing to do with the wholly undemocratic notion that citizens may tell educators how to conduct education and still less with the fantastic position that they may tell them how to live, vote, think, and speak.

In this country that strange phenomenon known as the alumni plays a weird and oftentimes a terrifying role. It is very odd, when you come to think of it, that people who have been the beneficiaries of an institution should think that they should control it, and for that very reason. If you think that the graduates believe they should control the university because they give money to it, I beg to disillusion you. The noise they make is in inverse proportion to the amount they give. The devotion of alumni is highly desirable. They can be useful in defending their alma mater from the public and in representing in their own persons the virtues for which it stands. Unfortunately their energies are often directed to quite other objects. They are interested in all the things that do not matter. And their oratorical powers and the hope that they may some day be induced to come forward with financial support intensify the interest of the university in the things that do not matter too. It is too much to expect that citizens who never went to college can understand what a university is when those upon whom the blessings of the higher learning have been showered understand it less well than anybody else. Any state university president will tell you that few things are so danger-

ous as an alumnus in the legislature. The presidents
of most endowed universities will tell you that the
most reactionary element in their constituencies is
their most vociferous graduates. Of course it is not
their fault. It is ours. Our confusion is so great that
we cannot make clear even to our own students what
we are trying to do.

Trustees are in a different category from alumni.
They at least have the undoubted legal right to control the institution. The wiser they are the less they
will attempt to do so. They are or ought to be more
competent than the faculty to manage property and
to interpret the university to the public. But a university that is run by its trustees will be badly run.
How can it be otherwise? Ordinarily the trustees are
not educators; usually they are nonresident. If they
are alumni, they must overcome the vices inherent
in that interesting group. If of their own motion
they take an educational problem in hand, they can
decide rightly only by accident.

The public may properly look to the trustees,
therefore, for the intelligent management of the institution, without imposing on the board the duty of
operating it in detail. The regents of a state university lately claimed the right to exclude the faculty

from the consideration of a certain subject on the ground that the regents were responsible for the university by law. But the general responsibility of trustees cannot run to the content of courses, the content of the curriculum, or the qualifications of the staff. These are technical matters that are beyond their competence. They should limit themselves to the selection of an administration that is competent to deal with these questions. If it turns out to be incompetent, they should get another. The attempt to take these matters into their own hands can only confound confusion.

To the love of money and a misconception of democracy I would add as a major cause of our disorder an erroneous notion of progress. I shall deal with the various aspects of this notion more at large in the three remaining chapters. I may mention them now by way of index. Our notion of progress is that everything is getting better and must be getting better from age to age. Our information is increasing. Our scientific knowledge is expanding. Our technological equipment in its range and excellence is far superior to what our fathers or even our older brothers knew.

Although the depression has shaken our faith a

little, we still remain true to the doctrine of progress and still believe in its universal application. Politics, religion, and even education are all making progress, too. In intellectual fields, therefore, we have no hesitancy in breaking completely with the past; the ancients did not know the things we know; they had never seen steam engines, or aëroplanes, or radios, and seem to have had little appreciation of the possibilities of the factory system. Since these are among the central facts in our lives, how can the ancients have anything to say to us?[1]

Descartes, Hume, and Rousseau, for example, did not find it in the least absurd that they should begin to think as though nobody had ever thought before. They did not even regard it as egotistical. It was merely natural; mankind had progressed to the point where it was necessary to cast out old errors and begin to develop a really intelligent program.

The tremendous strides of science and technology seemed to be the result of the accumulation of data. The more information, the more discoveries, the more inventions, the more progress. The way to promote progress was therefore to get more informa-

1. Cf. the recent remark of Sir R. W. Livingstone: "The Greeks could not broadcast the Æschylean trilogy, but they could write it."

tion. The sciences one by one broke off from philosophy and then from one another, and that process is still going on. At last the whole structure of the university collapsed and the final victory of empiricism was won when the social sciences, law, and even philosophy and theology themselves became empirical and experimental and progressive.

In some way or other the theory of evolution got involved in these developments; it gave aid and comfort to empiricism and was particularly happy in its effect upon education. Evolution proves, you see, that there is steady improvement from age to age. But it shows, too, that everybody's business is to get adjusted to his environment. Obviously the way to get adjusted to the environment is to know a lot about it. And so empiricism, having taken the place of thought as the basis of research, took its place, too, as the basis of education. It led by easy stages to vocationalism; because the facts you learn about your prospective environment (particularly if you love money) ought to be as immediate and useful as possible.

We begin, then, with a notion of progress and end with an anti-intellectualism which denies, in effect, that man is a rational animal. He is an animal and perhaps somewhat more intelligent than most. As such, a man can be trained as the more intelligent animals can be. But the idea that his education should consist of the cultivation of his intellect is, of course, ridiculous. What it must consist of is surveys, more or less detailed, of the modern industrial, technological, financial, political, and social situation so that he can fit into it with a minimum of discomfort to himself and to his fellow men. Thus the modern temper produces that strangest of modern phenomena, an anti-intellectual university.

Since an anti-intellectual university is a contradiction in terms, it is no wonder that the theories justifying it are very odd. There is, for instance, the great-man theory of education. Under this theory you pay no attention to what you teach, or indeed to what you investigate. You get great men for your faculty. Their mere presence on the campus inspires, stimulates, and exalts. It matters not how inarticulate their teaching or how recondite their researches; they are, as the saying goes, an education in themselves. This is a variant of the nauseating anecdote about Mark Hopkins on one end of the log and the student on the other.

Under any conditions that are likely to exist in

this country the log is too long and there are too many people sitting on both ends of it to make the anecdote apposite. Of course we should try to get great men into education, and each president should try to get as many of them as he can for his own faculty. But he can never hope to get very many, even if he knows one when he sees one. If a president succeeds in finding a few great men, he cannot hope to make them useful in an organization that ties them hand and foot and in a course of study that is going off in all directions at the same time and particularly in those opposite to the ones in which the great men are going. The fact is that the great-man theory is an excuse, an alibi, a vacuous reply to the charge that we have no intelligent program for the higher learning. It amounts to saying that we do not need one; we could give you one if we wanted to. But if you will only accept the great-man theory you will spare us the trouble of thinking.

Another theory we have developed is the character-building theory. It may be that we don't teach our students anything, but what of it? That isn't our purpose. Our purpose is to turn out well-tubbed young Americans who know how to behave in the

American environment.[2] Association with one another, with gentlemanly professors, in beautiful
buildings will, along with regular exercise, make our
students the kind of citizens our country needs.[3]
Since character is the result of choice it is difficult to
see how you can develop it unless you train the mind
to make intelligent choices. Collegiate life suggests
that the choices of undergraduates are determined
by other considerations than thought. Undoubtedly,
fine associations, fine buildings, green grass, good
food, and exercise are excellent things for anybody.
You will note that they are exactly what is advertised by every resort hotel. The only reason why they
are also advertised by every college and university is
that we have no coherent educational program to
announce.

2. See the remarks attributed to Father R. I. Gannon, President of
Fordham University, *New York Herald Tribune,* June 26, 1936, p. 21:
"From now on we must realize that the task of the university is to
graduate men of *contacts,* men whose social life has been developed
quite as earnestly as their funds of information, men who bear a definite and easily recognizable university stamp."

3. For a variation on this theme see an article in the *Yale Alumni
Weekly,* May 1, 1936, p. 7, in which the writer suggests that the curriculum is of little importance and that students really educate themselves best by informal association with one another and with professors. If this is true, there is no reason for worrying about what to
teach.

The character-building theory turned inside out is the doctrine that every young person ought to learn to work hard; and that it is immaterial what he works at as long as he has to work. Under the theory in this form the subject matter of legal study, for example, might just as well be botany or ornithology or any subject that is of such scope and difficulty as to require a substantial amount of hard labor. The prospective lawyer would have learned to work; anything else he must learn in practice anyway.

We shall all admit, I suppose, that learning how to work is perhaps the prime requisite for a useful life. It does seem unfortunate, however, that the higher learning can contribute nothing which clerking, coal-heaving, or choir practice cannot do as well or better. It is possible that apprenticing the young in some trade from the age of fourteen on might get the result here sought after with less expense and trouble. The hard-work doctrine would seem to be a defense-mechanism set up to justify our failure to develop anything worth working on.

The great-man theory and the character-building theory amount to a denial that there is or should be content to education. Those among us who assert that there is a content to education are almost unani-

mous in holding that the object of the higher learning is utility, and utility in a very restricted sense.
They write articles showing that the educated get
better jobs and make more money. Or they advocate
changes in education that will, they think, make it
more effective in preparing students to get better
jobs and make more money. Here we are brought
back to the love of money as a cause of our confusion. As the institution's love of money makes it
sensitive to every wave of popular opinion, and as
the popular opinion is that insofar as education has
any object it is economic, both the needs of the universities and the sentiments of the public conspire to
degrade the universities into vocational schools. To
these then a distorted notion of democracy leads us
to admit any and all students; for should not all our
youth have equal economic opportunities?

This is the position of the higher learning in
America. The universities are dependent on the
people. The people love money and think that education is a way of getting it. They think too that democracy means that every child should be permitted
to acquire the educational insignia that will be helpful in making money. They do not believe in the
cultivation of the intellect for its own sake. And the

distressing part of this is that the state of the nation determines the state of education.

But how can we hope to improve the state of the nation? Only through education. A strange circularity thus afflicts us.[4] The state of the nation depends on the state of education; but the state of education depends on the state of the nation. How can we break this vicious circle and make at last the contribution to the national life that since the earliest times has been expected of us? We can do so only if some institutions can be strong enough and clear enough to stand firm and show our people what the higher learning is. As education it is the single-minded pursuit of the intellectual virtues. As scholarship it is the single-minded devotion to the advancement of knowledge. Only if the colleges and universities can devote themselves to these objects can we look hopefully to the future of the higher learning in America.

4. On the difficulty of educating contrary to the prevailing views of society, see Plato, *Republic,* Book VI. And contrast Book IV: " 'And moreover,' said I, 'the state, if it once starts well, proceeds as it were in a cycle of growth. I mean that a sound nurture and education if kept up creates good natures in the state, and sound natures in turn receiving an education of this sort develop into better men than their predecessors. . . .' "

## II. THE DILEMMAS OF THE HIGHER LEARNING

THERE is a conflict between one aim of the university, the pursuit of truth for its own sake, and another which it professes too, the preparation of men and women for their life work. This is not a conflict between education and research. It is a conflict between two kinds of education. Both kinds are found in all parts of a university. As I shall show in a moment, professional training is given in almost every department, and the pursuit of truth for its own sake may occasionally be met with even in a professional school.

I need not tell you which of these two aims of the modern university has lately been more popular. A mere recital of the new schools, avowedly professional in purpose, that have appeared in the past thirty-five years will convince you that we have seen a dramatic shift in the composition of our universities. Since the beginning of the century the following units designed to fit students for specific occupations have appeared and have become respectable: schools of journalism, business, librarianship, social service, education, dentistry, nursing, forestry, diplomacy, pharmacy, veterinary surgery, and public administration. There are many others that have appeared, but have not yet become respectable. I have confined myself to what might be called the standard subjects.

These new schools, of course, consume a very large portion of the attention of students, faculty, and administrators. New developments in older professional disciplines are having the same effect. The growth of university medicine since 1910 has been phenomenal. The total assets contributing to medical education and research at the University of Chicago are more than forty million dollars, and medicine now consumes 25 per cent of the University's annual budget. Full-time faculties in law and engineering lead, of course, to greater expense than we were formerly put to; for part-time professors ordinarily carried away little or nothing as direct salary. In engineering the equipment becomes more elaborate as technology advances, and no end to the process is in sight. The modest requirements of a classics group of ten professors pale into insignificance beside the demands of the same number of engineers.

Emphasis on professionalism is further promoted by the increasing practice of pointing work from the junior year onward toward some professional school. The modern university is full of prelaw, prebusiness, predentistry, preëngineering, and premedical students whose course of study is determined by their professional ambitions. In some institutions the professional schools themselves begin with the junior year. This, as I shall show later, would be a sound organization under certain circumstances. Unfortunately those circumstances do not obtain today.

We find, moreover, that outside professional schools and in departments of arts, literature, and science the atmosphere in which the student labors is highly professional. Students do graduate work in organic chemistry because industry engages a large number of Ph.D.'s in this field every year. Students study for the M.A. because it is becoming necessary for positions in secondary schools. In the Middle West 45 per cent of the graduates of colleges of liberal arts go into teaching. In some colleges this proportion rises to 90 per cent. These colleges have been forced to offer the Master's degree so that their students may teach in secondary schools. They must also offer professional courses in education because state laws and accrediting agencies require such training for the prospective teacher at all levels of the public schools. In the universities students study for the Ph.D. because it is almost impossible to secure a college or university post without it. Seventy-five per cent of them have no interest in research; at least, that percentage never does any more after the exertions of the dissertation. It is hardly an exaggeration to say that university departments exist to train people to teach in university departments.

The pursuit of knowledge for its own sake is being rapidly obscured in universities and may soon be extinguished. Every group in the community that is well enough organized to have an audible voice wants the university to spare it the necessity of training its own recruits. They want to get from the university a product as nearly finished as possible, which can make as large and as inexpensive a contribution as possible from the moment of graduation. This is a pardonable, perhaps even a laudable, desire. But the effect of it on the universities will be that soon everybody in a university will be there for the purpose of being trained for something.

You may ask, what of it? You may suggest, and with reason, that the surroundings of a university are better than those in which the young practitioner might otherwise learn to practice. You may point out that a desirable uniformity may be obtained by insisting on educational requirements through which all neophytes must pass. You may say that the legal profession, for example, is not to be trusted with the education of the young lawyer; and if you do, you will, I am afraid, be right. My answer is that the burdens imposed upon the universities by this arrangement are bad for them and bad for the professions, and that the hope of doing a better job of training young people in the practices of a profession by having the universities do it is quite illusory.

It is plain enough, I suppose, that it is bad for the universities to vocationalize them. I do not deny that the professional atmosphere has an electrical effect on some students. I have seen Big Men at Yale, football heroes and social luminaries, wake up in the Law School under the stimulus of the incentives and competition of professional work. The close connection between law-school grades and law-office jobs and the fact that it is the fashion to work in law school accomplish a good many miracles of this variety. Undergraduate study can make no such appeal: it has no apparent connection with anything;

and the fashion of working at it would be difficult to start.

On the other hand, the vocational atmosphere is ruinous to attempts to lead the student to understand the subject. By hypothesis he is learning to practice the profession. You must, therefore, make clear to him at every step that the questions you are discussing have a direct bearing on his future experiences and on his success in meeting them. You must give him practical advice. A friend of mine recently took an hour to explain to his law-school class the economic and social background of the fellow-servant rule. At the end of the discussion one student inquired, "What's this got to do with the law?" There is a good deal to be said for the boy's position; he had come to the university under the impression that it would prepare him for the bar examinations and teach him the rules of the game. He felt that he was being cheated. Under these circumstances the temptation is irresistible to tell your students stirring anecdotes of your own days at the bar, to let them in on the tricks of the trade, and to avoid confusing their minds by requiring them to think about anything except what the courts will do.

The curriculum of such a school is what you

might expect it to be. It is confined to those subjects
which experience, tradition, or the state examinations have sanctified. The emphasis of the school is
determined by vocational pressures: if, for example,
big business is the thing, the course of study will re-
volve around commercial law. It is conceivable that
public law may take the place of commercial law if
the public service as an occupation continues to be a
popular topic of conversation. Criminal law, a subject of the greatest practical and theoretical importance, is required in law schools because nobody
would study it otherwise: there is in general no
money in it. Jurisprudence, which should be central
in any law curriculum, is studied by few and like
legal history is regarded as a peripheral or ornamen-
tal subject.

If you set out to prepare a boy for a trade there are
and can be no limits to the triviality to which you
will descend except those imposed by the limitations
on the time at your disposal. You can justify almost
anything on the ground that it may be helpful to the
young man in his profession. And if you take the
view that a university may properly prepare boys for
trades, there is no limit to the number of trades you
can train them for except those imposed by the

limitations on your resources. Since you can usually make a school pay if you make it vocational enough, there are really no limits at all. Any occupation that wishes to be dignified will say that it is a profession and suggest that the university coöperate by offering a curriculum preparing young people for it. This is a free country, which in my business means that anybody is free to make suggestions to a university and demand that they be carried out.

It follows that the professors in a university so conceived and so dedicated will be selected not because of their intellectual capacity, but because of the length, breadth, and depth of their practical experience. An ability to think and interest in thinking about the subject might be a handicap to a member of the staff. Although the salary scale in law schools is higher than in nonprofessional departments, the standard of scholarship is lower. In few other fields can a considerable reputation be grounded on the production of textbooks, manuals, or teaching materials. Moreover, a law teacher is supposed to be a good teacher first of all, which in professional schools is likely to mean a popular teacher. Sins of omission in scholarship are forgiven him if the boys agree that he knows the law. I have watched non-

lawyers come into law schools as professors and observed that the first thing they feel called on to do is
to act as though they had had brilliant careers at the
bar. In some cases they have thus defeated the object
of their appointment, which was to diminish rather
than increase the amount of vocational instruction.

These attitudes of students and teachers have re-
sulted in the isolation of professional schools from
the less frankly vocational elements in a university.
Whether other departments are actually pursuing
the truth for its own sake or not, they usually pretend that they are. The result is that there is hardly a
law school in the United States that is really part of
the university to which it nominally belongs. The
Yale Law School, indeed, has gone so far as to get
attached to the Harvard Business School and to co-
operate with it in a way in which it would never
think of doing with any Yale department, and in
which the Harvard Law School would never think
of doing with the Harvard Business School.

The Institute of Human Relations at Yale was an
attempt to unify certain professional and nonprofessional disciplines. The centrifugal forces at work
were so strong, however, that some elements were
blown out of the Institute at an early date; and in

spite of large resources and an elaborate plant the rest of the organization has been held together with some difficulty.

Superficially, at least, the law is connected with economics, ethics, politics, history, and psychology. Even in universities which have good departments in these fields the law school has little to do with them, and they have little to do with it. The engineering schools are notorious for their particularistic views of the natural sciences upon which engineering depends, and even of English composition, which, we are told, is something quite different in engineering from what it is in any other walk of life. Even in medical schools, which because of their organization into the clinical and preclinical years have a clearer notion of the relation of the sciences and the arts, you are likely to hear that a scientist outside the medical school can contribute little to medical progress and still less to medical education. If we assume that the professional disciplines have something that the rest of the university should know about and that the rest of the university might possibly shed some light on the professional disciplines, we must agree that isolation is bad for everybody. Indeed we can hardly make a case for including pro-

fessional schools in universities at all except on the
ground that mutual interchange with nonprofessional departments will give them something they
could not otherwise get.

Vocationalism leads, then, to triviality and isolation; it debases the course of study and the staff. It
deprives the university of its only excuse for existence, which is to provide a haven where the search
for truth may go on unhampered by utility or pressure for "results." I do not need to tell you how hard
it is in these times and in this country to keep this
characteristic activity of a university alive. There is,
as a matter of fact, no discernible enthusiasm for it
in the United States. Think where research in any
meaning of the word would be if it had not been for
the Rockefeller, Carnegie, and Harkness fortunes.
The spirit of the age is not congenial to long-term,
quiet investigations of matters which seem remote
from daily life; nor is it in fact congenial to the impartial, detached study of subjects that touch daily
life more nearly. Everybody wants the university to
advance his special brand of propaganda, to join his
private pressure group. He cannot imagine that the
university is not interested in pressure or propaganda. He assumes that if it is not with him it must

be against him. We have come to the point where the pursuit of truth for its own sake is actually regarded as dangerous by nervous newspaper publishers and worried business men.

Under these circumstances, we cannot cheerfully see the essential activity of a university submerged by wave after wave of vocationalism. But I suggest that vocationalism is not merely bad for the universities; it is bad also for the professions. I beg to lay down this fundamental proposition, that every profession requires for its continuous development the existence of centers of creative thought. To the extent to which universities and professional schools abandon creative thought and degenerate into trade schools the profession must degenerate into a trade. I attribute the decline of the church in this country to the decline of the theological schools, the plight of the law to the plight of the law schools, the condition of engineering to the condition of the engineering schools, and the comparative excellence of medicine to the comparative excellence of the medical schools developed since 1910.

If we examine those medical schools we see that they were made part of universities in order to secure for them the benefit of any thinking that might

be going on in them. The professors were to be in
the main men who could think about medicine.
Hence it was provided that they must have time to
do it. The number of students was to be small
enough to give the faculty opportunity to encourage
and direct the thinking of students. The emphasis
was not on hospital beds or on classroom facilities:
it was on laboratories. A connection was sought not
with large hospitals but with strong departments in
the basic sciences. Throughout all the modifications
which these schools have undergone, where close association with the basic sciences has been preserved,
their excellence has been maintained. Where those
departments have been weak or have become the
slaves of a professional group, the medical school has
deteriorated. It is not too much to say that an inti-
mate relationship with strong scientific departments
is the indispensable requirement for a strong medical school. Such a school may become strong tempo-
rarily through assembling a distinguished group of
clinicians and through the excellence of its supply of
clinical material. The pressure of clinical work is
such, however, that it becomes routine and the
school becomes routine if it is cut off from a center
of creative thought.

It is for this reason that the location of professional schools is of more significance than at first appears. Putting law schools near the courts and medical schools near the hospitals may have some advantages; they are nothing compared to the disadvantages of removing them from the university. Emphasis on the practical is not an emphasis that professional schools need. The demands of the profession are pressed upon them constantly. Only by a close association with a university can these demands be minimized and the emphasis placed where it needs to be, on the intellectual problems of the profession.

But location is not enough. Why is it that the clergy do not command the respect that we should all like to feel for them? I think you will find the answer by looking at the catalogue of any divinity school. It is now made up of subjects which, it is assumed, will assist the pastor in coping with his first charge. He learns about building management, and community singing, and church socials, and what is called religious education. Theology, which deals with the intellectual problems of his profession, has almost disappeared from the curriculum.

Why is it that American engineers do not in general rise to such commanding positions outside engineering practice as do the members of the profession in England? The answer is the relatively narrow vocational course of study which the American engineer must pursue. And if there are regrettable differences between the standards of the British bar and those of the American bar, is it not possible that one reason for them is that the American law school emphasizes training for the practice and the English universities emphasize understanding the law?

Turning professional schools into vocational schools degrades the universities and does not elevate the professions. I should also contend that it cannot accomplish the only purpose it can have, namely, the preparation of the student for the practice of his life work. It is, in short, bad for the student as well as for the universities and the professions.

My contention is that the tricks of the trade cannot be learned in a university, and that if they can be they should not be. They cannot be learned in a university because they get out of date and new tricks take their place, because the teachers get out of date and cannot keep up with current tricks, and because tricks can be learned only in the actual situation in which they can be employed.

I pass over the sad circumstance that a student

who spends his university career in specific vocational preparation and then does not go into the vocation has wasted his university career. Since 50 per
cent of engineering graduates do not become engineers, the engineering schools should try to give
them an education useful in any occupation instead
of teaching them tricks that are useful, if at all, only
in engineering.

All that can be learned in a university is the general principles, the fundamental propositions, the
theory of any discipline. The practices of the profession change so rapidly that an attempt to inculcate
them may merely succeed in teaching the student
habits that will be a disservice to him when he
graduates. Efforts to keep up with the current events
usually result in keeping up with the event before
last, so that I should not be surprised to learn that
law schools are just beginning to teach their students
how to proceed under N. R. A. The case method in
schools of business leads to the study of cases which
occurred during a boom, a year or so after a depression has set in. The practices of the practical world
are changing from day to day and even from hour to
hour. It is hard for the practitioner to keep up with
them, to say nothing of the professor removed from

the practical world. But suppose he can keep up with them; he has no guarantee that they will still be in vogue when his students seek to apply them. In fact he knows that the chances are that they will have disappeared and others which he failed to mention will have taken their place. Consider the feelings of a professor who drilled his students in the manipulation of the rules of common-law practice in Illinois, only to see them radically altered by the Practice Act.

What should he have taught them? He should have tried to see to it that they understood the principles, if any, of pleading. If they did they could have worked out for themselves the rationale of the rules of any jurisdiction; they might even understand the Illinois Practice Act.

You may say that the university medical school shows that both the principles and the practice of a profession may be learned in a university. The example of medicine is misleading. To make the example apposite to any other profession you would have to have two things which medicine has: first, a well-developed group of preclinical sciences in close association with the professional school, and second the actual conditions of practice on the university campus. The first of these some professional disciplines have, though they usually fail to make use of them. Engineering, for example, can find the physical sciences on the campus if it is willing to associate with them. Other professional branches, like the law, have nowhere to turn, for even if we assume that the social sciences are the sciences preclinical to the law, we cannot pretend that they are well worked out. They are, in fact, so badly worked out that at present it may be better for the law schools to stick to the law than to confuse themselves further by association with the social sciences.

The second of the requirements for achieving the results in training for practice that the medical school achieves is not enjoyed by any other professional unit. Only in medicine do we find the actual conditions of practice on the university campus. In the university medical school the professors are practicing medicine; their patients are suffering from diseases just as real as those which appear in any doctor's office. The student learns to practice in the only way in which anybody can learn to practice anything, by practicing. In law, engineering, journalism, business, and other real and imitation professional schools, the conditions of practice do not exist, and hence the student cannot learn to practice. If we were to attempt to get in law the same results that the medical school gets in medicine, we should have to organize the law school like a law office, with the professors practicing their profession, for a suitable fee, and the students learning as their assistants. Under the present system attempts to teach law students the art of practicing law will not succeed; they will, moreover, do positive harm, for they will divert the law student from what he might learn in law school, which is the theory, the fundamental propositions, the general principles of the law.

It is for this reason that "practical" work should not be attempted in professional schools even if it were possible to succeed with it: it interferes with the education of the student. It seems reasonably clear that a member of a learned profession should be educated. An educated man knows what he is doing and why. It is possible, I suppose, to be a very good cook without knowing any chemistry. At least the cookbooks confine themselves to telling you what to do under certain circumstances. It is not yours to reason why; you follow the instructions. It is perhaps for this reason that cooking has never been regarded as one of the learned professions. A man can be a good automobile driver, or bricklayer, or ditch digger on the same terms. All he needs to know is the rules of the trade. He does not need to understand them. But a profession cannot be truly learned unless its members understand the subject matter with which it deals.

The subject matter of a learned profession is intellectual. Though the rules of the trade may be learned in the practice, and indeed can only be learned there, the intellectual content of the profession can generally be mastered only in a university; at least a university should be the ideal place for such study. To the extent to which the attention of the student is directed to vocational interests and away from the intellectual content of the discipline the university fails to do the only thing it might do and attempts something in which it is bound to fail.

Yet we live in a world that is not merely unintellectual but anti-intellectual as well. Even the universities are anti-intellectual. The college, we say, is for social adaptation; the university is for vocational adjustment. Nowhere does insistence on intellectual problems as the only problems worthy of a university's consideration meet such opposition as in the universities themselves. We try to adjust students to life by giving them information about it, though we know the information will be archaic when they graduate. We try to adjust students to their life work by telling them how a professional man operates; we seldom bother to tell them why. The result is a course of study which is anti-intellectual from beginning to end.

A student may, then, enter a professional school without ever having been compelled to think, without, in short, being educated. In the same innocent condition he may enter a learned profession. We cannot wonder that the learned professions are no more learned than they are. If the student has not learned to think and if the technical procedures that have been taught him are of little value, what has he acquired in the professional school that could not be better learned elsewhere? As we saw at the beginning, he has learned to work. It is too bad that he has not been put to work on something worthwhile. If he had been, he might have been just as successful in the practice of his profession; for paradoxically enough a grasp of theory might enable him to meet practical situations which were overlooked or not foreseen by his instructors.

From this inspection of the universities we can see

what our dilemmas are. The first is the dilemma of professionalism. We do not feel safe in turning over education for the professions to the members of them. Universities are corporations not for profit, and can perhaps be trusted somewhat further. Many activities, such as public administration, are very important to the public. We see no way of preparing men to engage in them. The universities should be able to do something about this, too. Yet we know that a professional emphasis at present means a vocational emphasis and that such an emphasis is bad for the universities, bad for the professions, and bad for the students.[1]

Professionalism produces our second dilemma, which is the dilemma of isolation. To the extent to which professors are concerned with preparation for a specific trade they are isolated from professors interested in another specific trade, and both groups are isolated from those who are not interested in any trade at all but are attempting to pursue the truth for its own sake. On the other hand, all university departments with few exceptions are now engaged in

1. Cf. the recent observation of Dean C. H. Wilkinson, Worcester College, Oxford, "Specialism has largely taken the place of education and, with its twin brother professionalism, is spreading like a blight over the land."

professional training of some kind. The advantages of association with them are therefore highly dubious. University departments and professional schools now have no common frame of reference; it is possible that coöperation might increase confusion. An isolated vocational school can at least be certain that it is engaged in trying to prepare students for the vocation.

The third dilemma is that of anti-intellectualism. We are afflicted here again by the circularity of education and the national life. The professions and the public demand people trained according to their idea of what that training should be. How can their ideas be changed? Only by an education which they can get only in a university. Can a university train men for a profession in ways which the profession does not approve? Can a university make a profession learned in spite of itself? One of the chief concerns of a university department and *a fortiori* of a professional school is that its graduates shall get jobs. These departments and schools are not likely to break into a type of education with which the profession is unacquainted and of which it will be suspicious.

These dilemmas can, I think, be resolved; but it

will take another chapter to do it. I will say here by way of suggestion and summary that the dilemma of professionalism can be met in part by a thorough-going revision of our notions of what a profession is. From the university standpoint, at least, a professional discipline to be a professional discipline must have intellectual content, and have it in its own right. All there is to journalism can be learned through a good education and newspaper work. All there is to teaching can be learned through a good education and being a teacher. All there is to public administration can be discovered by getting a good education and being a public servant. As Aristotle said in the *Politics,* "The same education and the same habits will be found to make a good man and a good statesman and king." If the universities can revert to a condition where the number of professional schools and courses is limited to those that have intellectual content in their own right, they will have gone some distance toward disposing of the dilemma of professionalism.

They will go still farther toward disposing of it if they can insist that the professional schools and departments that remain deal with their subject matters in the true university spirit, that is, in the spirit of studying them for their own sake. Every learned profession has a great intellectual heritage, and it is this which should be the prime object of the attention of professional schools. I believe that these schools will find that their students will be better prepared for practice if they are trained to think in the subject matter of the professional discipline than if they have been taught by the cookbook method.

Studying professional subject matters in this spirit will produce better practitioners. It will also help to meet the dilemma of isolation. Subject to a qualification that I shall introduce later, the unifying principle of a university is the pursuit of truth for its own sake. So far as professional departments adopt this principle as their own they take their place in the university's community of scholars. If the number of professional groups can be limited to those that have intellectual content; if they and all other departments can conduct their work in the same spirit; if we can develop general education so that all advanced study will rest on a common body of knowledge, we may succeed in making our universities true communities and communities of true scholars.

Only by this route can we resolve the dilemma of

anti-intellectualism. If the leading universities can develop ideals which are intelligible to them; if they can adhere to them even if for a time they lose students and money, it may be that they can sometime make themselves and their ideals intelligible to our people. The justification for the privileges of universities is not to be found in their capacity to take the sons of the rich and render them harmless to society or to take the sons of the poor and teach them how to make money. It is to be found in the enduring value of having constantly before our eyes institutions that represent an abiding faith in the highest powers of mankind. The whole world needs this symbol now as never before. It is this symbol that I hope the American universities may become.

## III. GENERAL EDUCATION

MY excuse for devoting one chapter to general education in a series on the higher learning is the relation between the two. We can never get a university without general education. Unless students and professors (and particularly professors) have a common intellectual training, a university must remain a series of disparate schools and departments, united by nothing except the fact that they have the same president and board of trustees. Professors cannot talk to one another, not at least about anything important. They cannot hope to understand one another.

We may take it for granted that we shall always have specialists; yet neither the world nor knowledge of it is arbitrarily divided up as universities are. Everybody cannot be a specialist in every field. He must therefore be cut off from every field but his own unless he has the same basic education that other specialists have. This means more than having the same language and the same general interest in advancing knowledge. It means having a common stock of fundamental ideas. This becomes more important as empirical science advances and accumulates more and more data. The specialist in a narrow field has all he can do to keep up with the latest discoveries in it. Other men, even in his own department, struggling to stay abreast of what is happening in their own segments of the subject, cannot hope to keep up with what is happening in his. They may now expect to have some general understanding of what he is doing because they all have something in common; they are in the same department. But the day will shortly be upon us when even this degree of comprehension will be impossible, because of the infinite splitting of subject matters and the progressive submergence of any ideas by our insistence on information as the content of education.

Efforts to correct this tendency by administrative devices are mere palliatives. Roving professorships at Harvard, the divisional organization at Chicago, the Institute of Human Relations at Yale, noble and praiseworthy as they are, serve to mitigate and not to remove the disunity, discord, and disorder that have overtaken our educational system. If professors and students had a common stock of fundamental ideas, it might be possible for those in physiology to communicate with those in physics, and even law and divinity might begin to find it worthwhile to associate with one another.

In this chapter I should like to talk about content, not about method. I concede the great difficulty of communicating the kind of education I favor to those who are unable or unwilling to get their education from books. I insist, however, that the education I shall outline is the kind that everybody should have, that the answer to it is not that some people should not have it, but that we should find out how to give it to those whom we do not know how to teach at present. You cannot say my content is wrong because you do not know the method of transmitting it. Let us agree upon content if we can and have faith that the technological genius of America will solve the problem of communication.

Economic conditions require us to provide some kind of education for the young, and for all the young, up to about their twentieth year. Probably one-third of them cannot learn from books. This is no reason why we should not try to work out a better course of study for the other two-thirds. At the same time we should continue our efforts and experiments to find out how to give a general education to the hand-minded and the functionally illiterate. Even these attempts may be somewhat simplified if we know what a general education is.

Please do not tell me that the general education I propose should not be adopted because the great majority of those who pass through it will not go on to the university. The scheme that I advance is based on the notion that general education is education for everybody, whether he goes on to the university or not. It will be useful to him in the university; it will be equally useful if he never goes there. I will admit that it will not be useful to him outside the university in the popular sense of utility. It may not assist him to make money or to get ahead. It may not in any obvious fashion adjust him to his environment or fit him for the contemporary scene. It will, however, have a deeper, wider utility: it will cultivate the intellectual virtues.

The trouble with the popular notion of utility is that it confuses immediate and final ends. Material prosperity and adjustment to the environment are good more or less, but they are not good in themselves and there are other goods beyond them. The intellectual virtues, however, are good in themselves and good as means to happiness. By the intellectual virtues I mean good intellectual habits. The ancients

distinguish five intellectual virtues: the three speculative virtues of intuitive knowledge, which is the
habit of induction; of scientific knowledge, which is
the habit of demonstration; and of philosophical
wisdom, which is scientific knowledge, combined
with intuitive reason, of things highest by nature,
first principles and first causes. To these they add the
two virtues of the practical intellect: art, the capacity to make according to a true course of reasoning,
and prudence, which is right reason with respect to
action.[1]

In short, the intellectual virtues are habits resulting from the training of the intellectual powers. An
intellect properly disciplined, an intellect properly
habituated, is an intellect able to operate well in all
fields. An education that consists of the cultivation
of the intellectual virtues, therefore, is the most useful education, whether the student is destined for a
life of contemplation or a life of action. I would remind you of the words of Newman:

If then the intellect is so excellent a portion of us, and
its cultivation so excellent, it is not only beautiful, perfect,
admirable, and noble in itself, but in a true and high
sense it must be useful to the possessor and to all around

1. Cf. *Summa Theologica*, Part II, Q. 57, Art. 2–4.

him; not useful in any low, mechanical, mercantile sense, but as diffusing good, or as a blessing, or a gift, or power, or a treasure, first to the owner, then through him to the world.[2]

I shall not be attentive when you tell me that the plan of general education I am about to present is remote from real life, that real life is in constant flux and change, and that education must be in constant flux and change as well. I do not deny that all things are in change. They have a beginning, and a middle, and an end. Nor will I deny that the history of the race reveals tremendous technological advances and great increases in our scientific knowledge. But we are so impressed with scientific and technological progress that we assume similar progress in every field. We renounce our intellectual heritage, read only the most recent books, discuss only current events, try to keep the schools abreast or even ahead of the times, and write elaborate addresses on Education and Social Change.

Paul Shorey said:

If literature and history are a Heraclitean flux of facts, if one unit is as significant as another, one book, one

2. Cf. Aristotle, *Politics*, VIII, 3: "To be always seeking after the useful does not become free and exalted souls."

idea, the equivalent of another . . ., we may for a time
bravely tread the mill of scholastic routine, but in the end
the soul will succumb to an immense lassitude and baf-
flement. But if . . . the flux is not all, if the good, the
true, and the beautiful are something real and ascertain-
able, if these eternal ideals re-embody themselves from
age to age essentially the same in the imaginative visions
of supreme genius and in the persistent rationality and
sanity of the world's best books, then our reading and
study are redeemed, both from the obsessions of the hour,
and the tyranny of quantitative measures and mechanical
methods.

Our erroneous notion of progress has thrown the
classics and the liberal arts out of the curriculum,
overemphasized the empirical sciences, and made
education the servant of any contemporary movements in society, no matter how superficial. In recent
years this attitude has been accentuated by the
world-wide depression and the highly advertised political, social, and economic changes resulting from
it. We have been very much upset by all these things.
We have felt that it was our duty to educate the
young so that they would be prepared for further
political, social, and economic changes. Some of us
have thought we should try to figure out what the

impending changes would be and frame a curriculum that embodied them. Others have even thought that we should decide what changes are desirable and then educate our students not merely to anticipate them, but also to take part in bringing them about.

One purpose of education is to draw out the elements of our common human nature. These elements are the same in any time or place. The notion of educating a man to live in any particular time or place, to adjust him to any particular environment, is therefore foreign to a true conception of education.

Education implies teaching. Teaching implies knowledge. Knowledge is truth. The truth is everywhere the same.[3] Hence education should be everywhere the same. I do not overlook the possibilities of differences in organization, in administration, in local habits and customs. These are details. I suggest that the heart of any course of study designed for the whole people will be, if education is rightly understood, the same at any time, in any place, under any political, social, or economic conditions. Even the ad-

3. "It is therefore evident that, as regards the general principles whether of speculative or practical reason, truth or rectitude is the same for all, and is equally known by all," *Summa Theologica*, Part II, Q. 94, Art. 4.

ministrative details are likely to be similar because all societies have generic similarity.

If education is rightly understood, it will be understood as the cultivation of the intellect. The cultivation of the intellect is the same good for all men in all societies. It is, moreover, the good for which all other goods are only means. Material prosperity, peace and civil order, justice and the moral virtues are means to the cultivation of the intellect. So Aristotle says in the *Politics:* "Now, in men reason and mind are the end towards which nature strives, so that the generation and moral discipline of the citizens ought to be ordered with a view to them." An education which served the means rather than their end would be misguided.

I agree, of course, that any plan of general education must be such as to educate the student for intelligent action. It must, therefore, start him on the road toward practical wisdom. But the question is what is the best way for education to start him and how far can it carry him. Prudence or practical wisdom selects the means toward the ends that we desire. It is acquired partly from intellectual operations and partly from experience. But the chief requirement for it is correctness in thinking. Since education cannot duplicate the experiences which the student will have when he graduates, it should devote itself to developing correctness in thinking as a means to practical wisdom, that is, to intelligent action.

As Aristotle put it in the *Ethics,* ". . . while young men become geometricians and mathematicians and wise in matters like these, it is thought that a young man of practical wisdom cannot be found. The cause is that such wisdom is concerned not only with universals, but with particulars, but a young man has no experience, for it is length of time that gives experience." Since practical wisdom is "a true and reasoned capacity to act with regard to the things that are good or bad for man," it would seem that education can make its best contribution to the development of practical wisdom by concentrating on the reasoning essential to it.

A modern heresy is that all education is formal education and that formal education must assume the total responsibility for the full development of the individual. The Greek notion that the city educates the man has been forgotten. Everything that educated the man in the city has to be imported into our schools, colleges, and universities. We are beginning to behave as though the home, the church, the state, the newspaper, the radio, the movies, the neighborhood club, and the boy next door did not exist. All the experience that is daily and hourly acquired from these sources is overlooked, and we set out to supply imitations of it in educational institutions. The experience once provided by some of these agencies may be attenuated now; but it would be a bold man who would assert that the young person today lived a life less full of experience than the youth of yesterday. Today as yesterday we may leave experience to other institutions and influences and emphasize in education the contribution that it is supremely fitted to make, the intellectual training of the young. The life they lead when they are out of our hands will give them experience enough. We cannot try to give it to them and at the same time perform the task that is ours and ours alone.

Young people do not spend all their time in school. Their elders commonly spend none of it there. Yet their elders are, we hope, constantly growing in practical wisdom. They are, at least, having experience. If we can teach them while they are being educated how to reason, they may be able to comprehend and assimilate their experience. It is a good principle of educational administration that a college or university should do nothing that another agency can do as well. This is a good principle because a college or university has a vast and complicated job if it does what only it can do. In general education, therefore, we may wisely leave experience to life and set about our job of intellectual training.

If there are permanent studies which every person who wishes to call himself educated should master; if those studies constitute our intellectual inheritance, then those studies should be the center of a general education. They cannot be ignored because they are difficult, or unpleasant, or because they are almost totally missing from our curriculum today. The child-centered school may be attractive to the child, and no doubt is useful as a place in which the little ones may release their inhibitions and hence behave better at home. But educators cannot permit the students to dictate the course of study unless they are prepared to confess that they are nothing but chaperons, supervising an aimless, trial-and-error process which is chiefly valuable because it keeps young people from doing something worse. The free elective system as Mr. Eliot introduced it at Harvard and as Progressive Education adapted it to lower age levels amounted to a denial that there was content to education. Since there was no content to education, we might as well let students follow their own bent. They would at least be interested and pleased and would be as well educated as if they had pursued a prescribed course of study. This overlooks the fact that the aim of education is to connect man with man, to connect the present with the past, and to advance the thinking of the race. If this is the aim of education, it cannot be left to the sporadic, spontaneous interests of children or even of undergraduates.[4]

Mr. Gladstone once remarked that it is difficult to discern the true dimensions of objects in that mirage which covers the studies of one's youth. Even at stages beyond general education, when the student because he has had a general education and because he is more mature might be given wider latitude in selecting the subjects interesting to him, this can be permitted only to a limited degree. If there are an intellectual tradition and an intellectual inheritance

4. Plato, *Republic,* Book IX: " 'And it is plain,' I said, 'that this is the purpose of the law, which is the ally of all classes in the state, and this is the aim of our control of children, our not leaving them free before we have established, so to speak, a constitutional government within them and, by fostering the best element in them with the aid of the like in ourselves, have set up in its place a similar guardian and ruler in the child, and then, and then only we leave it free.' "

in the law, for example, law schools must see to it that they are transmitted to law students even if law students are more interested in the latest devices for evading the Sherman Antitrust Act.

It cannot be assumed that students at any age will always select the subjects that constitute education. If we permit them to avoid them, we cannot confer upon them insignia which certify to the public that they are in our opinion educated. In any field the permanent studies on which the whole development of the subject rests must be mastered if the student is to be educated.

The variations that should be encouraged fall not in the realm of content but in that of method. Allowances for individual differences should be provided for by abolishing all requirements except the examinations and permitting the student to take them whenever in his opinion he is ready to do so. The cultivation of independent thought and study, now almost wholly missing from our program, may thus be somewhat advanced. And this may be done without sacrificing the content of education to the obsessions of the hour or the caprices of the young.

If we are educators we must have a subject matter, and a rational, defensible one. If that subject matter is education, we cannot alter it to suit the whims of parents, students, or the public. Whewell, Master of Trinity College, Cambridge, one hundred years ago, said:

Young persons may be so employed and so treated, that their caprice, their self-will, their individual tastes and propensities, are educed and developed; but this is not Education. It is not the Education of a Man; for what is educed is not what belongs to man as man, and connects man with man. It is not the Education of a man's Humanity, but the Indulgence of his Individuality.

In general education we are interested in drawing out the elements of our common human nature; we are interested in the attributes of the race, not the accidents of individuals.

If our course of study reflects today an interest in the accidents of individuals; if the permanent studies are conspicuous by their absence from it, I can only say that these are the reasons why our course of study is bad. We know that our course of study leads to the most unfortunate results in the organization of education, in the qualities and activities of professors and students, and in the cultivation of our people. It is surely not a criticism of the permanent studies that they have had no share in producing these results.

By insisting on the permanent studies as the heart of a general education I do not mean to insist that they are the whole of it. We do not know enough to know whether certain technological work, for example, may not have a certain subsidiary value in general education for some students. Nor do I overlook the fact that since by hypothesis general education may be terminal for most students, it must connect them with the present and future as well as with the past. It is as important for them to know that thinking is still going on as it is for them to know what has been thought before.

The question whether certain technical work shall be allowed to be a part of general education is rather a question of method than of content, a question how to teach rather than what. Technology as such has no place in general education. If it can be justified at all, it can only be because we discover that certain principles can best be communicated through technical work. The question of present thought is largely answered by saying that it is impossible to think of a teacher who contented himself with eluci-

dating the thought of the past without intimating
that these ideas have a history running to the present day.

The proponents of current events as the subject
matter of education gain little by insisting on the importance of present thought; for they are not much
interested in thought of any kind. They would be
only less horrified if contemporary thought were
made the heart of general education than they would
be if St. Augustine or Spinoza were central in it.
They would get little consolation from the remarks
of Whewell about what he called the progressive
studies, which were to make their first appearance
at a much later stage of education than the one we
are here considering. He said:

It is not enough that we take for this purpose any ex-
pression of the present activities of men's minds. Progressive studies, too, must be a part of the development
of humanity in its general form. They must express an
activity which belongs to man as man. They must be,
though not permanent in their form, universal in their
principles. They must be the results, not of individual
caprice, or fancy, but of human Reason. They must aim,
not at mere change or novelty, but at Truth. And since
the progress of the human mind is from Truth to Truth,

the new Truths must be founded upon the old ones. The progressive studies which education embraces must rest upon the permanent studies which it necessarily includes. The former must be its superstructure, the latter, its foundation.

Again he says:

A man who really participates in the progress of the sciences, must do so by following their course when the time of education is past. . . . Modern Science and Philosophy ought to be introduced into education so far as to show their nature and principles; but they do not necessarily make any considerable or definite part of it. The intellectual culture, though it will be incomplete if these are excluded, may still be a culture which connects him with the past, and prepares him for the present; but an education from which classical literature or mathematical reasoning is omitted, however familiar it may make a man with the terms of modern literature and philosophy, must leave him unprepared to understand the real purport of literature and philosophy, because he has not the intellectual culture which the greatest authors in literature and philosophy have always had.[5]

5. Consider the importance to English law of Aristotle's distinctions of misadventure, mistake, an act of injustice, and the unjust act of an unjust man. *Ethics*, 1135b. Consider also the influence on Anglo-Saxon jurisprudence of Locke's *Second Essay on Civil Government*.

Let us avoid all questions of administration and method. Let us assume that we have an intelligible organization of education under which there is a four-year unit, beginning at about the beginning of the junior year in high school and ending at about the end of the sophomore year in college. Let us assume that we are going to try to teach in that unit everybody who can learn from books. Let us assume further that the conclusion of their work in this unit will mark the end of formal instruction for most students. They will not go on to the university. Nevertheless we must have a curriculum which will, in the main, do as well for those who are going on as those who are not. What shall this curriculum be?

We have excluded body building and character building. We have excluded the social graces and the tricks of trades. We have suggested that the curriculum should be composed principally of the permanent studies. We propose the permanent studies because these studies draw out the elements of our common human nature, because they connect man with man, because they connect us with the best that man has thought, because they are basic to any further study and to any understanding of the world. What are the permanent studies?

They are in the first place those books which have through the centuries attained to the dimensions of classics. Many such books, I am afraid, are in the ancient and medieval period. But even these are contemporary. A classic is a book that is contemporary in every age. That is why it is a classic. The conversations of Socrates raise questions that are as urgent today as they were when Plato wrote. In fact they are more so, because the society in which Plato lived did not need to have them raised as much as we do. We have forgotten how important they are.

Such books are then a part, and a large part, of the permanent studies. They are so in the first place because they are the best books we know. How can we call a man educated who has never read any of the great books in the western world? Yet today it is entirely possible for a student to graduate from the finest American colleges without having read any of them, except possibly Shakespeare. Of course, the student may have heard of these books, or at least of their authors. But this knowledge is gained in general through textbooks, and textbooks have probably done as much to degrade the American intelligence as any single force. If the student should know about Cicero, Milton, Galileo, or Adam Smith, why should he not read what they wrote? Ordinarily what he knows about them he learns from texts which must be at best second-hand versions of their thought.

In the second place these books are an essential part of general education because it is impossible to understand any subject or to comprehend the contemporary world without them. If we read Newton's *Principia,* we see a great genius in action; we make the acquaintance of a work of unexampled simplicity and elegance. We understand, too, the basis of modern science. The false starts, the backing and filling, the wildness, the hysteria, the confusion of modern thought and the modern world result from the loss of what has been thought and done by earlier ages. The Industrial Revolution begins our study of history and the social sciences. Philosophy begins with Descartes and Locke and psychology with Wundt and William James. Natural science originates with the great experimenters of the nineteenth century. If anything prior is mentioned, it is only as a reminder that our recent great achievements in these fields must, of course, have had some primitive beginnings in the dark earlier centuries. The classics, if presented at all, are offered in excerpts out of context, and for the most part for the sake of showing the student how far we have progressed beyond our primitive beginnings.

Yet we may with profit remember the words of Nicholas Murray Butler:

Only the scholar can realize how little that is being said and thought in the modern world is in any sense new. It was the colossal triumph of the Greeks and Romans and of the great thinkers of the Middle Ages to sound the depths of almost every problem which human nature has to offer, and to interpret human thought and human aspiration with astounding profundity and insight. Unhappily, these deep-lying facts which should be controlling in the life of a civilized people with a historical background, are known only to a few, while the many grasp, now at an ancient and well-demonstrated falsehood and now at an old and well-proved truth, as if each had all the attractions of novelty.

You will note that Mr. Butler says that only a scholar can realize these things. Why should this insight be confined to scholars? Every educated person should know the colossal triumph of the Greeks and Romans and the great thinkers of the Middle Ages. If every man were educated—and why should he not be?—our people would not fall so easily a prey to

the latest nostrums in economics, in politics, and, I
may add, in education.

You will observe that the great books of the western world cover every department of knowledge.
The *Republic* of Plato is basic to an understanding
of the law; it is equally important as education for
what is known as citizenship. The *Physics* of Aristotle, which deals with change and motion in nature,
is fundamental to the natural sciences and medicine,
and is equally important to all those who confront
change and motion in nature, that is, to everybody.
Four years spent partly in reading, discussing, and
digesting books of such importance would, therefore, contribute equally to preparation for special-
ized study and to general education of a terminal variety. Certainly four years is none too long for this
experience. It is an experience which will, as I have
said, serve as preparation for advanced study and as
general education designed to help the student understand the world. It will also develop habits of
reading and standards of taste and criticism that will
enable the adult, after his formal education is over,
to think and act intelligently about the thought and
movements of contemporary life. It will help him to
share in the intellectual activity of his time.

In order to read books one must know how to do it. The degeneracy of instruction in English grammar should not blind us to the fact that only through grammatical study can written works be understood. Grammar is the scientific analysis of language through which we understand the meaning and force of what is written. Grammar disciplines the mind and develops the logical faculty. It is good in itself and as an aid to reading the classics. It has a place in general education in connection with the classics and independently of them. For those who are going to learn from books learning the art of reading would seem to be indispensable.

I do not suggest that learning the languages or the grammar in which the ancient classics were written is necessary to general education. Excellent translations of almost all of them now exist. Unless it can be shown that the study of Greek and Latin grammar is essential to the study of English grammar or that the mastery of the Greek and Latin languages is essential to mastery of our own, I see no reason for insisting on these languages as part of general education. The modern languages, of course, are no necessary part of it. Time should be allowed for students to acquire them; but the examinations reflecting general education should not contain them. They are an extracurriculum accomplishment or a tool for advanced work rather than a fundamental portion of general education.

I add to grammar, or the rules of reading, rhetoric and logic, or the rules of writing, speaking, and reasoning. The classics provide models of excellence; grammar, rhetoric, and logic are means of determining how excellence is achieved. We have forgotten that there are rules for speaking. And English composition, as it is commonly taught, is a feeble and debased imitation of the classical rules of writing, placing emphasis either on the most trivial details or on what is called self-expression. Self-expression as here understood is, of course, the exact reverse of the discipline which rhetoric in all ages up to the present was used to give. Logic is a statement in technical form of the conditions under which reasoning is rigorously demonstrative. If the object of general education is to train the mind for intelligent action, logic cannot be missing from it.

Logic is a critical branch of the study of reasoning. It remains only to add a study which exemplifies reasoning in its clearest and most precise form. That study is, of course, mathematics, and of the mathe-

matical studies chiefly those that use the type of ex-
position that Euclid employed. In such studies the
pure operation of reason is made manifest. The subject matter depends on the universal and necessary
processes of human thought. It is not affected by differences in taste, disposition, or prejudice. It refutes
the common answer of students who, conformable to
the temper of the times, wish to accept the principles
and deny the conclusions. Correctness in thinking
may be more directly and impressively taught
through mathematics than in any other way.[6] It is
depressing that in high schools and junior colleges
mathematics is not often taught in such a way as to
achieve these ends. Arithmetic and geometry are
there usually presented to the student as having great
practical value, as of course they have.[7] But I have
had students in the freshman year in college who
had never heard that they had any other value, and

6. " 'You see, then, my friend,' said I, 'that this branch of study
really seems to be indispensable for us, since it plainly compels the soul
to employ pure thought with a view to truth itself.' " Plato, *Republic*,
Book VII.

7. Plato on geometers: "Their language is most ludicrous, though
they cannot help it, for they speak as if they were doing something
and as if all their words were directed toward action. For all their
talk is of squaring and applying and adding and the like, whereas the
real object of the entire study is pure thought." *Ibid.*, Book VII. See
also Aristotle, *Ethics*, 1098a.

who were quite unwilling to consider mathematical questions until their practical possibilities had been explained. To this pass has our notion of utility brought us.

We have then for general education a course of study consisting of the greatest books of the western world and the arts of reading, writing, thinking, and speaking, together with mathematics, the best exemplar of the processes of human reason. If our hope has been to frame a curriculum which educes the elements of our common human nature, this program should realize our hope. If we wish to prepare the young for intelligent action, this course of study should assist us; for they will have learned what has been done in the past, and what the greatest men have thought. They will have learned how to think themselves. If we wish to lay a basis for advanced study, that basis is provided. If we wish to secure true universities, we may look forward to them, because students and professors may acquire through this course of study a common stock of ideas and common methods of dealing with them. All the needs of general education in America seem to be satisfied by this curriculum.

What, then, are the objections to it? They cannot

be educational objections; for this course of study appears to accomplish the aims of general education. One objection may be that the students will not like it, which is, as we have seen, irrelevant. But even if it were relevant, it is not true. Since the proposed curriculum is coherent and comprehensible, and since it is free from the triviality that now afflicts our program, students will respond to it if the teachers will give them a chance to do it.

It may be said that the course of study is too difficult. It is not too difficult for students who can read or who can be taught to do so. For ease of reading, as well as other qualities, *The Federalist,* an American classic, is superior to some recent treatises on government and public administration; Herodotus is more sprightly than most modern historians of the ancient world; and Plato and Aristotle are as intelligible as contemporary philosophers.

No, the students can do the work if the faculties will let them. Will the faculties let them? I doubt it. The professors of today have been brought up differently. Not all of them have read all the books they would have to teach. Not all of them are ready to change the habits of their lives. Meanwhile they are bringing up their successors in the way they

were brought up, so that the next crop will have
the habits they have had themselves. And the love
of money, a misconception of democracy, a false
notion of progress, a distorted idea of utility, and
the anti-intellectualism to which all these lead conspire to confirm their conviction that no disturb-
ing change is needed. The times call for the estab-
lishment of a new college or for an evangelistic
movement in some old ones which shall have for its
object the conversion of individuals and finally of
the teaching profession to a true conception of general education. Unless some such demonstration or
some such evangelistic movement can take place, we
shall remain in our confusion; we shall have neither
general education nor universities; and we shall continue to disappoint the hopes of our people.

## IV. THE HIGHER LEARNING

WE have now examined the external conditions under which American education operates. We have seen what the dilemmas of the higher learning are. We have seen that they may be resolved in part by developing a general education. We have seen what a general education is. Our object is now to discover what, given general education, the higher learning should be.

Let me make clear at the outset that I am here considering the university as an educational institution. I yield to no one in my admiration for and belief in the accumulation of data, the collection of facts, and the advance of the empirical sciences. These taken together constitute one of the grand activities of modern times. It must be continued and encouraged. I wish merely to point out that this activity must be conducted in such a way as not to confuse or prevent that intellectual training and development which in my view are education. How this may be done I shall hope to show later.

I know, of course, that thinking cannot proceed

divorced from the facts and from experience. All questions of organization and management, however, are questions of emphasis. By emphasizing the intellectual content of education I do not mean to minimize the importance of the collection of data.[1] I do mean to put it in its proper place. That place is, in any intelligible scheme of higher education, a subordinate one.

I beg to call attention in this connection to two meanings of the word research. Research in the sense of gathering data for the sake of gathering them has, as I shall show, no place in a university. Research in the sense of the development, elaboration, and refinement of principles together with the collection and use of empirical materials to aid in these processes is one of the highest activities of a university and one in which all its professors should be engaged.

Let me say, too, that I concede the probable necessity in some fields of practical training which the young man or woman should have before being

1. De Tocqueville, *Democracy in America,* Part II, First Book, Ch. X, "In the present age the human mind must be coerced into theoretical studies; it runs of its own accord to practical applications; and, instead of perpetually referring it to the minute examination of secondary effects, it is well to divert it from them sometimes, in order to raise it up to the contemplation of primary causes."

permitted to engage in the independent practice of a profession. Since by definition this training cannot be intellectual, and since by definition a university must be intellectual, this type of specific preparation for specific jobs cannot be conducted as part of the university's work. How it may be conducted without interfering with university education I shall suggest as we proceed.

Under an intelligible program of general education, the student would come to the end of the sophomore year with a solid knowledge of the foundations of the intellectual disciplines. He would be able to distinguish and think about subject matters. He would be able to use language and reason. He would have some understanding of man and of what connects man with man. He would have acquired some degree of wisdom.

On his emergence from general education what would he find? He would find a vast number of departments and professional schools all anxious to give him the latest information about a tremendous variety of subjects, some important, some trivial, some indifferent. He would find that democracy, liberalism, and academic freedom meant that all these subjects and fractions of subjects must be regarded as equally valuable. It would not be democratic to hint that Scandinavian was not as significant as law or that methods of lumbering was not as fundamental as astronomy. He would find a complete and thoroughgoing disorder.

He would find, too, that we were proud of this disorder and resisted attempts to correct it by calling them undemocratic and authoritarian.[2] As the free elective system denies that there is content to education, so the organization of the modern university denies that there is rationality in the higher learning. The free elective system as applied to professors means that they can follow their own bents, gratify their own curiosity, and offer courses in the results. The accumulation of credits in these courses must lead, like those in any other courses, to the highest academic degrees. Discrimination among courses would be undemocratic. The student would, then, confront an enormous miscellany, composed principally of current or historical investigations in a terrifying multiplicity of fields.

2. Cf. the remarks of Judge Learned Hand to the Harvard alumni, June 18, 1936: "There is no democracy among human values, however each may cry out for an equal vote. It is the business of the soul to impose her own order upon the clamorous rout; to establish a hierarchy appropriate to the demands of her own nature . . ."

He would find that these collections were offered him on either of two assumptions, or both: one, that they were good in themselves, or two, that they would train him for something. They are good in themselves because they are the results of the pursuit of truth for its own sake. They will train him for something because they are the latest reports from the front on which he will have to fight the battle of life. He would find, to his surprise, that the schools and departments offering to prepare him for the learned professions were somewhat less learned than the rest and that their courses of study did not indicate where or what the learning was that made the profession learned. He would find that the other departments that wanted to train him wanted to train him to be a technician or a practitioner or a person who knew how to make the observations, scientific or historical, which they were making themselves.

He would find an especially strange mixture in the field of what might be called the productive arts. He would discover in the natural sciences that making a highly refined gadget to make highly refined measurements was as important as the development of a new theory of the cosmos. He would find that making music, sculpture, or painting was as much a university discipline as theology. But he would discover that the Fine Arts, under the influence of the empirical sciences and the popular notion of pursuing the truth for its own sake, had become an empirical, historical, and "scientific" discipline, too. The microscopic study of Byzantine mosaics to determine their age and lineage by looking at their teeth, as it were, is as important as understanding them; in fact it is more so, because such investigation is "scientific research," and understanding is not.

This is what the young man would see as he stood gazing across the threshold of the higher learning. It may be briefly described as chaos. Who would blame him if, after one look, he decided to go into the comparative order and sanity of the business world?

How can these things be? Why is it that the chief characteristic of the higher learning is disorder? It is because there is no ordering principle in it. Certainly the principle of freedom in the current sense of that word will not unify it. In the current use of freedom it is an end in itself. But it must be clear that if each person has the right to make and achieve his own choices the result is anarchy and the dissolution of the whole. Nor can we look to the pursuit of truth for its own sake to unify the higher learning. Philistines still ask, what is truth? And all truths cannot be equally important. It is true that a finite whole is greater than any of its parts. It is also true, in the common-sense use of the word, that the New Haven telephone book is smaller than that of Chicago. The first truth is infinitely more fertile and significant than the second. The common aim of all parts of a university may and should be the pursuit of truth for its own sake. But this common aim is not sufficiently precise to hold the university together while it is moving toward it. Real unity can be achieved only by a hierarchy of truths which shows us which are fundamental and which subsidiary, which significant and which not.

The modern university may be compared with an encyclopedia. The encyclopedia contains many truths. It may consist of nothing else. But its unity can be found only in its alphabetical arrangement. The university is in much the same case. It has departments running from art to zoology; but neither the students nor the professors know what is the relation of one departmental truth to another, or what the relation of departmental truths to those in the domain of another department may be.

The medieval university had a principle of unity. It was theology. The medieval theologians had worked out an elaborate statement in due proportion and emphasis of the truths relating to man and God, man and man, and man and nature. It was an orderly progression from truth to truth. As man's relations to God were the highest of which he could conceive; as all his knowledge came from God and all his truths, the truths concerning God and man were those which gave meaning and sequence to his knowledge. Theology ordered the truths concerning man and man; humanism was theocentric; man loved his brothers in God.[3] Theology ordered the truths of man and nature, for God created the world; he created man to live in it, and placed him in definite relation to other creatures. The insight that governed the system of the medieval theologians was that as first principles order all truths in the speculative order, so last ends order all means and actions in the practical order. God is the first truth and the last end. The medieval university was rationally ordered, and, for its time, it was practically ordered, too.

3. *Summa Theologica,* Part II, Q. 2, Art. 7, "But man is not to be loved for his own sake, but whatever is in man is to be loved for God's sake."

But these are other times; and we are trying to discover a rational and practical order for the higher learning of today. Theology is banned by law from some universities. It might as well be from the rest. Theology is based on revealed truth and on articles of faith. We are a faithless generation and take no stock in revelation. Theology implies orthodoxy and an orthodox church. We have neither. To look to theology to unify the modern university is futile and vain.

If we omit from theology faith and revelation, we are substantially in the position of the Greeks, who are thus, oddly enough, closer to us than are the Middle Ages. Now Greek thought was unified. It was unified by the study of first principles. Plato had a dialectic which was a method of exploring first principles. Aristotle made the knowledge of them into the science of metaphysics. Among the Greeks, then, metaphysics, rather than theology, is the ordering and proportioning discipline. It is in the light of metaphysics that the social sciences, dealing with man and man, and the physical sciences dealing with man and nature, take shape and illuminate one another. In metaphysics we are seeking the causes of the things that are. It is the highest science, the first

science, and as first, universal. It considers being as
being, both what it is and the attributes which be-
long to it as being.

The aim of higher education is wisdom. Wisdom
is knowledge of principles and causes. Metaphysics
deals with the highest principles and causes. Therefore metaphysics is the highest wisdom. So much is
this the case that Aristotle feels called on to refer to
the suggestion that this knowledge must be confined
to God. He says:

But the divine power cannot be jealous, nor should any
other science be thought more honorable than one of this
sort. For the most divine science is also most honorable,
and this science alone must be, in two ways, most divine.
For the science which it would be most meet for God to
have is a divine science, and so is any science that deals
with divine objects; and this science alone has both these
qualities; for (1) God is thought to be among the causes
of all things and to be a first principle, and (2) such a
science either God alone can have or God above all
others.

It is a science which is divine in the sense that Aristotle elsewhere concludes that happiness is divine: it
is not beyond nature and reason; it is widely dif-
fused and accessible to all who are capable of virtue.

Metaphysics, then, as the highest science, ordered the thought of the Greek world as theology ordered that of the Middle Ages. One or the other must be called upon to order the thought of modern times. If we cannot appeal to theology, we must turn to metaphysics. Without theology or metaphysics a unified university cannot exist.

Both are almost totally missing today. And with them has gone any intelligible basis for the study of man in his relations with other men. The truths of ethics, for example, are now merely common-sense teachings about how to get along in the world. Morals degenerate into the mores unless they have a higher meaning imparted to them by theology or metaphysics.[4]

A similar degeneration overtakes natural science. If the world has no meaning, if it presents itself to us as a mass of equivalent data, then the pursuit of truth for its own sake consists of the indiscriminate accumulation of data. We cannot understand it;

4. Kant, *Fundamental Principles of the Metaphysic of Ethics* (10th ed.), p. 5, "A metaphysic of morals is therefore indispensably necessary, not merely for speculative reasons, in order to investigate the sources of the practical principles which are to be found *a priori* in our reason, but also because morals themselves are liable to all sorts of corruption, as long as we are without that clue and supreme canon by which to estimate them correctly."

there is no need to try. Whether we can understand the world or not, however, we can seek to master it. That is a useful and a popular thing to do. But its educational and scientific consequences are vocationalism, empiricism, and disorder; and its moral consequences are an immoral morality. As a contemporary has said:

In order to reign as a demi-urge over nature, man in his intelligence and in his life must in reality subordinate himself to inhuman and technical necessities and to the energies of the natural order which, originally placed in operation by him, are now invading the human mind. . . . Whatever the acquired gains may be from other points of view, the conditions. of life of the human being are thus becoming more and more inhuman. . . . Behold man the center of the world, a world all the parts of which are inhuman and press against him. . . . In such a morality, not man nor human life as such, but agents exterior to man, material forces, instruments of human life, are subjected to reason. . . . This morality does not liberate man but on the contrary weakens him, dispossesses him, and makes him slave to all the atoms of the universe, and above all to his own misery and egoism. What remains of man? A consumer crowned with science. That is the last gift, the twentieth century gift of the Cartesian reformation.

We believe, then, that if we can gather enough information about the world we can master it. Since we do not know precisely which facts will prove to be helpful, we gather them all and hope for the best. This is what is called the scientific spirit. From our study of man and nature this notion has extended to our study of man and man. Power becomes the great word in political science; and the prediction of what the courts will do takes the place of justice as the object of the lawyer and the legal scholar. The scientific spirit leads us to accumulate vast masses of data about crime, poverty, unemployment, political corruption, taxation, and the League of Nations in our quest for what is known as social control. A substantial part of what we call the social sciences is large chunks of such data, undigested, unrelated, and meaningless.

The study of man and nature and of man and man has thus sunk under waves of empiricism and vocationalism. Saddest of all is the fate that has overtaken theology itself. Displaced from its position as the queen of the sciences, it now finds itself a feeble imitator of all the rest. In general its students are its students in name only. They are actually studying history or languages or experimental psychology or

the empirical social sciences or even the empirical
natural sciences, trying to find a place for a church
and a religion that know no theology. They employ
the information thus gained for vocational purposes:
they hope it may adjust them to their professional
environment. The institutional church, religious
education, and the training of various types of "lead-
ers" for religious, semireligious, or nonreligious or-
ganizations occupy more and more of the attention
of the divinity schools. How to Conduct a Business
Men's Forum on Public Affairs may shortly be a
more important section of the curriculum than theology. Theology has now been degraded to the bot-
tom of the educational hierarchy. Its nominal fol-
lowers, frightened out of their wits by the scientific
spirit, have thrown theology overboard and have
transferred their affections to those overdressed hoy-
dens, the modern versions of the natural and social
sciences.

With theology has gone metaphysics. It is now but
a shrunken shadow of its former self. It makes an
attenuated appearance in a department called philosophy, by the creation of which we apparently
mean to indicate that philosophy has nothing to do
with what is studied in the rest of the university. Yet

it is impossible to keep metaphysics completely out of the consideration of any subject.[5] For example, the science of physics, as Newman has pointed out, requires the admission of certain metaphysical postulates, if it is to be more than a theory or hypothesis; as, for instance, that what happened yesterday will happen tomorrow; that there is such a thing as matter, that our senses are trustworthy, that there is a logic of induction, and so on. So metaphysics comes back all over the campus and in sadly mutilated condition. For example, a class studying *Faust* will engage in arguments about the metaphysical problems raised by the work. This discussion is objectionable because neither the teacher nor the class is competent to participate in it and because it results in failure to consider *Faust* as a poem, a drama, and a work of art. If the teacher and the class had had some metaphysical training they could, if they liked, discuss intelligently the metaphysics of Goethe; but what is more important, their knowledge of the first principles of æsthetics would enable them to consider the artistic merits of the play. You

5. Cf. the dilemma suggested by Aristotle: "You say one must philosophize. Then you must philosophize. You say one must not philosophize. Then (to prove your contention) you must philosophize. In any case you must philosophize."

will have noticed, too, that it has become almost a tradition in this country for a natural scientist after he achieves eminence and leisure to employ some of both in metaphysical, and even theological, speculations. Without any particular training in these disciplines and with a healthy contempt for those who have he proceeds to confuse the public further about the greatest questions that have confronted the human mind.

The reception accorded the expressions of these gentlemen shows how much we feel the need of an orthodox theology or a systematic metaphysics. So strong is this feeling that not infrequently we find the nonfiction best seller of the year serving as a contemporary Holy Writ. Carrel's *Man the Unknown* seems to be taking this part at the moment, as Durant's *Story of Philosophy* did a few years ago.

In the one country in the modern world where God has been officially abolished as the basis of theology or as a first principle in metaphysics, we have seen a furious effort on the part of the government to supply something in His place. Karl Marx is the new God. Dialectical materialism is the new theology. We may say in behalf of the Marxists that they at least realize that there is no advance in the speculative realm which does not have practical consequences, and no change in the practical realm which need not be speculatively analyzed. They realize that it is impossible to have social order without intellectual order.[6]

I am not here arguing for any specific theological or metaphysical system. I am insisting that consciously or unconsciously we are always trying to get one. I suggest that we shall get a better one if we recognize explicitly the need for one and try to get the most rational one we can. We are, as a matter of fact, living today by the haphazard, accidental, shifting shreds of a theology and metaphysics to which we cling because we must cling to something. If we can revitalize metaphysics and restore it to its place in the higher learning, we may be able to establish rational order in the modern world as well as in the universities.

If this miracle could be performed, what would the educational content of the higher learning be,

6. Cf. the insistence of Lenin on the importance of theory, especially in *Our Programme* and *What Is To Be Done?* In the latter, p. 584 in *The Handbook of Marxism,* he says: "The case of the Russian Social-Democrats strikingly illustrates the fact observed in the whole of Europe . . . that the notorious freedom of criticism implies, not the substitution of one theory by another, but freedom from every complete and thought-out theory; it implies eclecticism and absence of principle."

and what would a university be like? The student beginning with the junior year would study metaphysics, the science of first principles. He would study the social sciences, which are practical sciences, dealing with the relations of man and man. He would study natural science, which is the science of man and nature. He would study all three categories, with emphasis, if you like, on one of them. He would study them in relation to one another. It is clear that they deal with the same propositions and facts, but with different ultimate references. The student would study them without any vocational aim; that is, the subject matter would be the same for those who were planning to enter a learned profession and those who were not. The study would not proceed from the most recent observations back to first principles, but from first principles to whatever recent observations were significant in understanding them. I remind you of the distinction between the permanent and the progressive studies that we made in discussing general education. The higher learning is concerned primarily with thinking about fundamental problems. "A man who really participates in the progress of the sciences, must do so when the time of education is past." In the university he must come to grips with fundamental problems; for he can only do it there. He will have time enough later to keep up with current events.

The fundamental problems of metaphysics, the social sciences, and natural science are, then, the proper subject matter of the higher learning. These categories are exhaustive. I have used the word metaphysics to include not only the study of first principles, but also all that follows from it, about the principles of change in the physical world, which is the philosophy of nature, and about the analysis of man and his productions in the fine arts including literature. The social sciences embrace the practical sciences of ethics, politics, and economics, together with such historical and empirical materials as may be needed to supplement them for the guidance of human action. The theoretical principles of ethics, politics, and economics are, of course, principles of speculative philosophy. The principles of ethics, theoretically considered, are to be found in metaphysics. In ethics itself the same knowledge is viewed in the practical order. To speak of ethics, politics, and economics as practical philosophy is to indicate that they are philosophical knowledge organized for the sake of action. In the law we have a practical application of this body of practical principles. By the natural sciences I mean, of course, the study of nature. The natural sciences derive their principles from the philosophy of nature, which in turn depends on metaphysics. In the study of them such recent observations as serve to illustrate, exemplify, or confirm these principles must be included. Medicine and engineering are applications of this whole body of knowledge.

By constructing a university in this way it can be made intelligible. Metaphysics, the study of first principles, pervades the whole. Inseparably connected with it is the most generalized understanding of the nature of the world and the nature of man. Dependent on this and subordinate to it are the social and natural sciences. In due subordination in the teaching of these we include historical and current empirical material. Such material ceases to be the whole of these sciences as studied in a university and becomes instead an aid in understanding their principles. In a university like this it should be possible to get an education; it is possible to get one in no other way, for in no other way can the world of thought be presented as a comprehensible whole.

I should insist that a university is concerned with thought and that the collection of information, historical or current, had no place in it except as such data may illustrate or confirm principles or assist in their development. It is perfectly clear, however, that the mere collection of information is of great importance and that it must be carried on somewhere. It is useful and economical, perhaps even essential, to have it carried on in part under the auspices and protection of universities and in connection with them. Moreover, in dealing with social questions it is important to provide a refuge for men who can and will study them in as detached, objective, and impartial a manner as possible. The more acute and controversial the question is, the more important is the provision of a refuge for its discussion. Discussions of such questions cannot, however, occupy the central place in education at any of the levels we have been considering. They can enter it only as exemplifying or illuminating the principles of the social sciences.

So information on subjects important to the public should be gathered, analyzed, and published. Public administration, public education, social service, taxation, inflation, etc., are all subjects of this type. They are at what may be called the research level rather than the educational. They should be studied; they may be studied in connection with a university. But their inclusion in the university curriculum accomplishes, as we have seen, no contribution to it except to intensify its disorder.

In the same way men who are collecting information in the natural sciences, which is a highly desirable thing to do, should, though they have no place in the university proper, find a haven in connection with it. Industry is not now prepared, and probably never will be, to conduct or finance this work on any adequate scale. I suggest, therefore, that research institutes be established at universities, in which all the current and historical facts now collected by professors, and more, can be assembled. The members of these institutes would not be members of the university faculties, unless they were also working on fundamental problems in metaphysics, social science, and natural science. Men working on such problems, and only these, would have a voice in matters affecting the conduct of the university and the content of its work.

If the learned professions cannot be trusted to communicate the practices of the professions to the young, it may be desirable in certain cases also to attach to the university on the same terms technical institutes in which the student may become familiar with these routines. Even here, of course, some care should be exercised to see to it that the routines are worthy and susceptible of communication.

The research institutes will be technical institutes to a certain extent; for they will train people to carry on research of the type that they carry on themselves. It is conceivable that some technical institutes will do some research, of the kind, naturally, that is thought to assist in technical training.

The departmental system, which has done so much to obstruct the advancement of education and the advancement of knowledge, will vanish. The three faculties will constitute the entire organization of the university. Members of existing departments who are exclusively concerned either with data collecting or vocational training will be transferred to research or technical institutes. Only those who are working on fundamental problems in the fields of the three faculties will remain as professors in the university.

The professional schools of the university would disappear as such. Education for the learned professions would be conducted in the three faculties of metaphysics, social science, and natural science, with prospective clergymen graduating under the faculty of metaphysics, lawyers under that of social science, and doctors and engineers under that of natural science. Studying under the faculty of metaphysics we should expect to find prospective philosophers, too; under that of the social sciences future administrators, judges, legislators, statesmen, and men of affairs; and under that of natural science those destined for a life of scientific investigation. Those professional schools which have no intellectual content in their own right would disappear altogether, except as their activities might be thought worthy of preservation in research or technical institutes.

To illustrate the possibilities of this type of education I may refer in greater detail to education for the learned professions. The prospective clergyman would come to the end of his sophomore year with a good general education derived from the classics and the liberal arts. In the university he would spend the greater part of his time under the faculty of metaphysics. But he would also study ethics, politics, economics, and law, though not in the same way nor to the same extent as the prospective lawyer. Although he would acquire some familiarity with the leading ideas of natural science, he would not need much in this field beyond what is supplied by metaphysics itself. If it were desirable or necessary for him to learn certain ministerial habits before he could be trusted with a congregation, he might acquire them either through a system of apprenticeship or in a technical institute established near the university for the purpose.

The future doctor would come to the university with precisely the same general education as his clerical colleague. He would study metaphysics and the philosophy of nature. By this study he might be disciplined in such a way that he would not be given to sophomoric philosophical speculations in his idle hours. He would learn from it, too, to see the leading principles underlying all the experimental natural sciences. After this his predominant occupation would be with the physical and biological sciences as preclinical. Although he would also get an understanding of the social sciences and law, he would not study them in great detail. The necessary experience that he must have before he could be trusted with a patient should be secured in an institute attached to the university and to a hospital.

The prospective lawyer would have exactly the same general education as the clergyman and the doctor. He would study metaphysics, because without it ethics, politics, and economics are meaningless. He would get this philosophical training for the sake of his major occupation: the mastery of jurisprudence, which consists of ethics and politics and the philosophy of law based upon them. He would also study the empirical and historical knowledge of society, the history of law and legal institutions, economics and economic history. These he would need for the casuistical application of principles to legal cases. He would gain some knowledge of the physical world, but would require little more than he would get from metaphysics. Anything further that he needed for the practice of his profession, such as familiarity with the rules of a particular jurisdiction, with methods of using digests and reports, with drafting legal documents, with writing briefs, or with the tricks of the trade, he might acquire in a legal institute attached to the university.

The prospective teacher's general education would be identical with that of the lawyer, doctor, and clergyman. With a good education in the liberal arts, which are grammar, rhetoric, logic, and mathematics, he has learned the basic rules of pedagogy. The liberal arts are, after all, the arts of reducing the intellect from mere potentiality to act. And this is what teaching is. The liberal arts train the teacher in how to teach, that is, in how to organize, express, and communicate knowledge. In the university he should learn what to teach. He should study under all three faculties, and especially under that of metaphysics. If it then appears that he is destined for investigation or for vocational instruction he may learn the techniques of investigation or practice in a research or technical institute. If, for example, he seems likely to be a school administrator, and if a school administrator should know the number of janitors per cubic foot that school buildings require, and if a school administrator should not be trusted with a school unless he has this knowledge, then this knowledge should be gained in a technical institute.

It is only by educating teachers in this way that we shall ever break the vicious circle to which I have many times referred—the circle in which the products of a bad system grow up to the operators and perpetuators of it. If we can begin with the education of a few teachers we may hope that gradually through the years a general education and a university may emerge.

In summary, then, the university would consist of the three faculties, metaphysics, social science, and natural science. The professors would be those who were thinking about the fundamental problems in these fields. The teaching would be directed to understanding the ideas in these fields, and would have no vocational aim. The student would study all three subject matters, with emphasis upon one. He would enter upon this program at the beginning of the junior year and continue in it for about three years.

Since it is desirable that the collection of historical and current data should proceed in the vicinity of the university, research institutes in the social and natural sciences may be established in connection with it, though not as part of it. Technical institutes in the same relation to the university may also be created if needed to give practical training for occupations which require a background of special knowledge and facility in special techniques. Students should in no case be admitted to technical or research institutes until they have completed their general and higher education.

We see, then, that we may get order in the higher learning by removing from it the elements which disorder it today, and these are vocationalism and unqualified empiricism. If when these elements are removed we pursue the truth for its own sake in the light of some principle of order, such as metaphysics, we shall have a rational plan for a university. We shall be able to make a university a true center of learning; we shall be able to make it the home of creative thought.

We see, too, that in such a university the dilemmas of the higher learning are resolved. The dilemma of professionalism cannot obstruct us, because no distinction is made between the professional and nonprofessional disciplines. They are all studied in the three faculties and studied in the same way. Training in the techniques of the profession is left to the profession or, if necessary, to technical institutes so organized as not to confuse the university.

For somewhat similar reasons the dilemma of isolation will also cease from troubling. Disciplines will not be isolated from one another; they will be united, and by a rational principle. Professors and students will all be pursuing the truth for its own sake; they will know what truths to pursue and why. Since all students will study under all the faculties, the education they acquire will not be piecemeal or miscellaneous; it will be as unified as the university itself.

Even the dilemma of anti-intellectualism is easier to deal with. Anti-intellectualism is so much a part of the temper of the times that it will be difficult to meet this dilemma as squarely or satisfactorily as we can meet the other two. The university that I have been describing is intellectual. It is wholly and completely so. As such, it is the only kind of university worth having. I believe that it will accomplish greater political and professional results than one that is devoted to current events or vocational training.

If the country is not prepared to believe these things, it can get what it wants through the technical and research institutes I have proposed. They are so planned as to draw off the empiricism and vocationalism that have been strangling the universities and to leave them free to do their intellectual job.

If we can secure a real university in this country and a real program of general education upon which its work can rest, it may be that the character of our civilization may slowly change. It may be that we can outgrow the love of money,[7] that we can get a saner conception of democracy, and that we can even understand the purposes of education. It may be that we can abandon our false notions of progress and utility and that we can come to prefer intelligible organization to the chaos that we mistake for liberty. It is because these things may be that education is important. Upon education our country must pin its hopes of true progress, which involves scientific and technological advance, but under the direction of reason; of true prosperity, which includes external goods but does not overlook those of the soul; and of true liberty, which can exist only in society, and in a society rationally ordered.

7. Aristotle, *Politics*, II, 7: "For it is not the possessions but the desires of mankind which require to be equalized, and this is impossible, unless a sufficient education is provided by the state."